U.S. POLICY TOWARD ROGUE NATIONS

Other books in the At Issue series:

U.S. POLICY TOWARD ROGUE NATIONS

James D. Torr, *Book Editor*

Bonnie Szumski, *Publisher*
Scott Barbour, *Managing Editor*
Helen Cothran, *Senior Editor*

AT **ISSUE**

OPPOSING VIEWPOINTS® SERIES

GREENHAVEN PRESS®

THOMSON
™
GALE

San Diego • Detroit • New York • San Francisco • Cleveland
New Haven, Conn. • Waterville, Maine • London • Munich

For more information, contact
Greenhaven Press
27500 Drake Rd.
Farmington Hills, MI 48331-3535
Or you can visit our Internet site at http://www.gale.com

LIBRARY OF CONGRESS CATALOGING-IN-PUBLICATION DATA

U.S. policy toward rogue nations / James D. Torr, book editor.
   p. cm. — (At issue)
Includes bibliographical references and index.
ISBN 0-7377-2196-0 (lib. : alk. paper) — ISBN 0-7377-2197-9 (pbk. : alk. paper)
   1. United States—Foreign relations. 2. United States—Military policy.
3. Terrorism. 4. Aggression (International law). 5. Subversive activities.
I. U.S. policy toward rogue nations. II. Torr, James D., 1974– . III. At issue (San Diego, Calif.)
JZ1480.U15 2004
327.73—dc22   2003062480

Contents

Introduction

The term "rogue nation" was first adopted by the U.S. government in the 1990s under President Bill Clinton to describe nations that were considered to pose a threat to the United States. The term was controversial from the start, as many world leaders and critics within the United States did not feel it was appropriate for the U.S. government to label entire nations as villainous. Responding partly to such criticisms, in June 2000 the Clinton administration adopted the term "countries of concern" in place of "rogue nations."

Soon after President George W. Bush took office in 2001, the term "rogue nation" was readopted. One year after the September 11, 2001, terrorist attacks on America, the Bush White House issued a formal definition of the term in its *National Security Strategy of the United States of America*. "In the 1990s we witnessed the emergence of a small number of rogue states that . . . share a number of attributes," states the document, these states:

- brutalize their own people and squander their national resources for the personal gain of the rulers;

- display no regard for international law, threaten their neighbors, and callously violate international treaties to which they are party;

- are determined to acquire weapons of mass destruction, along with other advanced military technology, to be used as threats or offensively to achieve the aggressive designs of these regimes;

- sponsor terrorism around the globe; and

- reject basic human values and hate the United States and everything for which it stands.

In his 2002 State of the Union address, though he did not use the term "rogue nation," President Bush singled out three countries—North Korea, Iran, and Iraq—as members of an "axis of evil":

> North Korea is a regime arming with missiles and weapons of mass destruction, while starving its citizens. Iran aggressively pursues these weapons and exports terror, while an unelected few repress the Iranian people's hope for freedom. Iraq continues to flaunt its hostility toward America and to support terror. . . . States like these, and their terrorist allies, constitute an axis of evil, arming to threaten the peace of the world.

In addition to these three countries, the Department of State's 2002 *Pat-*

terns of Global Terrorism identifies four other nations as state sponsors of terrorism: Cuba, Libya, Syria, and Sudan.

U.S. policy toward rogue nations in a global context

Even more controversial than the definition of the term "rogue nation" is the question of how the United States should deal with countries that sponsor terrorism or pursue the development of biological, chemical, or nuclear weapons. Americans hold a variety of opinions on whether the United States should use diplomacy, economic sanctions, or even military action against rogue nations. An important consideration in these debates is that fact that how the United States chooses to deal with rogue nations affects not just its own national security, but also the complex issue of America's role in the international community.

For most of the last half of the twentieth century, international relations were dominated by the Cold War. The United States and its allies stood for democracy and free-market capitalism, while the Soviet Union and its allies represented communism. Though the danger of war between the two superpowers was always present, the struggle between them lent a degree of order to international relations. With the fall of the Soviet Union in 1991, the international community was left searching for, as the first President Bush put it in his January 1991 State of the Union speech, a "new world order."

In February 1991, the international community was forced to deal with the rogue nation of Iraq which, under the dictatorship of Saddam Hussein, had invaded the neighboring nation of Kuwait the previous August. The United States and the United Nations immediately demanded that Iraq withdraw from Kuwait, and the United States began deploying troops in Saudi Arabia. In the following weeks President Bush helped forge a coalition of twenty-eight nations chartered by the United Nations to drive Iraqi forces from Kuwait. U.S. and Allied forces launched the ground war on Kuwait on February 23, and by February 27 the Iraqi occupation army had been driven from Kuwait. On March 31, Iraq accepted the terms of a cease-fire agreement under which Saddam Hussein was allowed to remain in power in Iraq.

Although the term "rogue nation" had not yet been coined, the 1991 Persian Gulf War demonstrated that states such as Iraq, which was armed with chemical weapons and willing to defy international law, posed a great threat to peace in the post–Cold War era. In the first Iraq war, the United States acted multilaterally, as part of a coalition of many nations. The successful cooperation between the United States and the United Nations in the 1991 Gulf War led many experts to believe that such cooperation would become the norm in policing rogue nations in the post–Cold War era. However, twelve years later, in March 2003, the United States again invaded Iraq, with the aid of the United Kingdom but in the face of strong opposition from France, Germany, and Russia, and without the express sanction of the United Nations. This unilateral action against Iraq has raised questions about whether the United States will also seek to use military action against other rogue nations, and if so, whether it will respect the authority of the United Nations. In other words, will the United States act alone in policing rogue nations, or in concordance with the global community of nations?

Preemptive war against rogue nations: the case of Iraq

The United States invaded Iraq in 2003 to bring down the regime of Saddam Hussein. U.S. officials believed Iraq was developing weapons of mass destruction (WMD) in violation of UN regulations instituted after the first Iraq war, and that these weapons might be used either by Iraq or terrorist groups. Much of the opposition to the invasion stemmed from the fact that Iraq had not actually used weapons of mass destruction since the 1991 Persian Gulf War. As well, there was only limited evidence that Saddam Hussein had a WMD development program. The U.S. decision to invade Iraq was based largely on the Bush administration's doctrine of preemptive war.

President Bush first described the doctrine of preemptive war at a June 2002 speech at the U.S. Military Academy at West Point, New York. Referring primarily to Saddam Hussein's suspected WMD development programs, the president warned that

> We cannot defend America and our friends by hoping for the best. . . . If we wait for threats to fully materialize, we will have waited too long. . . . We must take the battle to the enemy, disrupt his plans, and confront the worst threats before they emerge. . . . Our security will require all Americans to be forward-looking and resolute, to be ready for preemptive action when necessary.

Bush's doctrine of preemption was further described in the September 2002 *National Security Strategy:* "As was demonstrated by the losses on September 11, 2001, mass civilian casualties is the specific objective of terrorists and these losses would be exponentially more severe if terrorists acquired and used weapons of mass destruction. . . . To forestall or prevent such hostile acts by our adversaries, the United States will, if necessary, act preemptively."

Critics of the Bush doctrine of preemption see it as a declaration that the United States will attack any nation it perceives to be a threat, without regard for international law or the United Nations. For example, Harvard University professor Stanley Hoffman writes that the Bush *National Security Strategy*

> presumes that the United States is the sole judge of the legitimacy of its own or anyone else's preemptive strikes. . . . It promises to maintain whatever military capability is needed to defeat any attempt by any state to impose its will on the United States or its allies, and to dissuade potential adversaries from building up their own forces. . . . In context, it amounts to a doctrine of global domination.

When the United States invaded Iraq in 2003 despite UN opposition, many critics saw this as confirmation of Hoffman's charges.

An American empire?

Even before the 2003 invasion of Iraq was underway, both supporters and critics of the invasion were asking what rogue nation would be the next target in America's war against terrorism. Some of the possibilities include

North Korea, which has been suspected of trying to develop nuclear weapons since the early 1990s, and Iran, Syria, and other Middle Eastern nations that have long been suspected of supporting terrorists. Critics of the Iraq invasion worry that it might be the first in a series of wars designed to eliminate any threats these nations pose to the United States. British political commentator Matthew Parris writes, "I am afraid that [the invasion of Iraq] will prove to be the first in an indefinite series of American interventions. I am afraid this is the beginning of a new empire."

The concept of an American empire has become a major theme in discussions of U.S. policy toward rogue nations. For many people, the concept of empire is wholly un-American. The United States was founded, after all, on a rejection of British imperial rule. Imperialism contradicts the American belief that people should govern themselves through democratic institutions. "Until very recently," says Columbia University professor Bruce Robbins, "there was no way you could use the word 'empire' in any but a critical sense. It's been a very, very long American tradition to set ourselves apart from the European notion of empire."

Supporters of an American empire argue that it would be different from the empires of the past. While the British empire of the nieteenth century served largely to bolster Great Britain's economy, they argue, the goals of an American empire will be to spread democracy and protect the world from rogue nations. "The Europeans fought to subjugate 'natives'; Americans will fight to bring them democracy and the rule of law," writes former *Wall Street Journal* editor Max Boot. Boot and others believe that the U.S. invasion of Iraq should serve as a starting point for establishing democracy in the Middle East:

> The September 11 attack was a result of *insufficient* American involvement [in the Middle East]. . . . Once we have deposed Saddam, we can impose an American-led, international regency in Baghdad. . . . This could be the chance . . . to establish the first Arab democracy.

Boot has called this effort "liberal imperialism," but others reject the term "imperialism" entirely. "Imperialism means conquest, acquisition—subjugating and taking over some other people and territory for one's own enrichment and aggrandizement—and the United States is not considering doing that for a second," says foreign policy scholar Joshua Muravchik. "Exporting democracy is completely different."

Empire or not, the Unites States is the world's most powerful nation, in both military and economic terms, and Iraq will not be the last nation to threaten its interests. How the United States chooses to deal with rogue nations—unilaterally or multilaterally, peacefully or through military action, forcing regime change or exporting democracy—will have profound consequences for its security as well as its role within the global community of nations.

1

The United States Should Prevent Rogue Nations from Obtaining Weapons of Mass Destruction

George W. Bush

George W. Bush is the forty-third president of the United States. He took office on January 20, 2001. The White House released the following document in December 2002.

The United States must not permit nations that are hostile to the United States to develop or acquire nuclear, chemical, or biological weapons of mass destruction (WMD). To prevent rogue nations from developing WMD, the United States and its allies should employ interdiction—the interception and confiscation of materials used to build WMD—and deterrence—the threat of massive retaliation from U.S. military forces in response to a WMD attack. The United States may also need to employ preemptive military strikes to eliminate imminent WMD threats. Finally, the United States and its allies should also encourage international nonproliferation and arms reduction agreements.

Weapons of mass destruction (WMD)—nuclear, biological, and chemical—in the possession of hostile states and terrorists represent one of the greatest security challenges facing the United States. We must pursue a comprehensive strategy to counter this threat in all of its dimensions.

An effective strategy for countering WMD, including their use and further proliferation, is an integral component of the National Security Strategy of the United States of America. As with the war on terrorism, our strategy for homeland security, and our new concept of deterrence, the U.S. approach to combat WMD represents a fundamental change from the past. To succeed, we must take full advantage of today's opportunities, including the application of new technologies, increased emphasis on intel-

George W. Bush, *The National Strategy to Combat Weapons of Mass Destruction*, December 2002, pp. 1–6.

ligence collection and analysis, the strengthening of alliance relationships, and the establishment of new partnerships with former adversaries.

Weapons of mass destruction could enable adversaries to inflict massive harm on the United States, our military forces at home and abroad, and our friends and allies. Some states, including several that have supported and continue to support terrorism, already possess WMD and are seeking even greater capabilities, as tools of coercion and intimidation. For them, these are not weapons of last resort, but militarily useful weapons of choice intended to overcome our nation's advantages in conventional forces and to deter us from responding to aggression against our friends and allies in regions of vital interest. In addition, terrorist groups are seeking to acquire WMD with the stated purpose of killing large numbers of our people and those of friends and allies—without compunction and without warning.

We will not permit the world's most dangerous regimes and terrorists to threaten us with the world's most destructive weapons. We must accord the highest priority to the protection of the United States, our forces, and our friends and allies from the existing and growing WMD threat.

Pillars of our national strategy

Our National Strategy to Combat Weapons of Mass Destruction has three principal pillars:

Counterproliferation to Combat WMD Use. The possession and increased likelihood of use of WMD by hostile states and terrorists are realities of the contemporary security environment. It is therefore critical that the U.S. military and appropriate civilian agencies be prepared to deter and defend against the full range of possible WMD employment scenarios. We will ensure that all needed capabilities to combat WMD are fully integrated into the emerging defense transformation plan and into our homeland security posture. Counterproliferation will also be fully integrated into the basic doctrine, training, and equipping of all forces, in order to ensure that they can sustain operations to decisively defeat WMD-armed adversaries.

We will not permit the world's most dangerous regimes and terrorists to threaten us with the world's most destructive weapons.

Strengthened Nonproliferation to Combat WMD Proliferation. The United States, our friends and allies, and the broader international community must undertake every effort to prevent states and terrorists from acquiring WMD and missiles. We must enhance traditional measures—diplomacy, arms control, multilateral agreements, threat reduction assistance, and export controls—that seek to dissuade or impede proliferant states and terrorist networks, as well as to slow and make more costly their access to sensitive technologies, material, and expertise. We must ensure compliance with relevant international agreements, including the Nuclear Nonproliferation Treaty (NPT), the Chemical Weapons Convention

(CWC), and the Biological Weapons Convention (BWC). The United States will continue to work with other states to improve their capability to prevent unauthorized transfers of WMD and missile technology, expertise, and material. We will identify and pursue new methods of prevention, such as national criminalization of proliferation activities and expanded safety and security measures.

Consequence Management to Respond to WMD Use. Finally, the United States must be prepared to respond to the use of WMD against our citizens, our military forces, and those of friends and allies. We will develop and maintain the capability to reduce to the extent possible the potentially horrific consequences of WMD attacks at home and abroad.

The three pillars of the U.S. national strategy to combat WMD are seamless elements of a comprehensive approach. Serving to integrate the pillars are four cross-cutting enabling functions that need to be pursued on a priority basis: intelligence collection and analysis on WMD, delivery systems, and related technologies; research and development to improve our ability to respond to evolving threats; bilateral and multilateral cooperation; and targeted strategies against hostile states and terrorists.

Counterproliferation

We know from experience that we cannot always be successful in preventing and containing the proliferation of WMD to hostile states and terrorists. Therefore, U.S. military and appropriate civilian agencies must possess the full range of operational capabilities to counter the threat and use of WMD by states and terrorists against the United States, our military forces, and friends and allies.

Interdiction. Effective interdiction is a critical part of the U.S. strategy to combat WMD and their delivery means. We must enhance the capabilities of our military, intelligence, technical, and law enforcement communities to prevent the movement of WMD materials, technology, and expertise to hostile states and terrorist organizations.

Deterrence. Today's threats are far more diverse and less predictable than those of the past. States hostile to the United States and to our friends and allies have demonstrated their willingness to take high risks to achieve their goals, and are aggressively pursuing WMD and their means of delivery as critical tools in this effort. As a consequence, we require new methods of deterrence. A strong declaratory policy and effective military forces are essential elements of our contemporary deterrent posture, along with the full range of political tools to persuade potential adversaries not to seek or use WMD. The United States will continue to make clear that it reserves the right to respond with overwhelming force—including through resort to all of our options—to the use of WMD against the United States, our forces abroad, and friends and allies.

In addition to our conventional and nuclear response and defense capabilities, our overall deterrent posture against WMD threats is reinforced by effective intelligence, surveillance, interdiction, and domestic law enforcement capabilities. Such combined capabilities enhance deterrence both by devaluing an adversary's WMD and missiles, and by posing the prospect of an overwhelming response to any use of such weapons.

Defense and Mitigation. Because deterrence may not succeed, and because of the potentially devastating consequences of WMD use against our forces and civilian population, U.S. military forces and appropriate civilian agencies must have the capability to defend against WMD-armed adversaries, including in appropriate cases through preemptive measures. This requires capabilities to detect and destroy an adversary's WMD assets before these weapons are used. In addition, robust active and passive defenses and mitigation measures must be in place to enable U.S. military forces and appropriate civilian agencies to accomplish their missions, and to assist friends and allies when WMD are used.

U.S. military forces . . . must have the capability to defend against WMD-armed adversaries, including in appropriate cases through preemptive measures.

Active defenses disrupt, disable, or destroy WMD en route to their targets. Active defenses include vigorous air defense and effective missile defenses against today's threats. Passive defenses must be tailored to the unique characteristics of the various forms of WMD. The United States must also have the ability rapidly and effectively to mitigate the effects of a WMD attack against our deployed forces.

Our approach to defend against biological threats has long been based on our approach to chemical threats, despite the fundamental differences between these weapons. The United States is developing a new approach to provide us and our friends and allies with an effective defense against biological weapons.

Finally, U.S. military forces and domestic law enforcement agencies as appropriate must stand ready to respond against the source of any WMD attack. The primary objective of a response is to disrupt an imminent attack or an attack in progress, and eliminate the threat of future attacks. As with deterrence and prevention, an effective response requires rapid attribution and robust strike capability. We must accelerate efforts to field new capabilities to defeat WMD-related assets. The United States needs to be prepared to conduct post-conflict operations to destroy or dismantle any residual WMD capabilities of the hostile state or terrorist network. An effective U.S. response not only will eliminate the source of a WMD attack but will also have a powerful deterrent effect upon other adversaries that possess or seek WMD or missiles.

Nonproliferation

Active Nonproliferation Diplomacy. The United States will actively employ diplomatic approaches in bilateral and multilateral settings in pursuit of our nonproliferation goals. We must dissuade supplier states from cooperating with proliferant states and induce proliferant states to end their WMD and missile programs. We will hold countries responsible for complying with their commitments. In addition, we will continue to build coalitions to support our efforts, as well as to seek their increased support for nonproliferation and threat reduction cooperation programs. However, should our wide-ranging nonproliferation efforts fail, we must have available the full range of operational capabilities necessary to defend against the possible employment of WMD.

Multilateral Regimes. Existing nonproliferation and arms control regimes play an important role in our overall strategy. The United States will support those regimes that are currently in force, and work to improve the effectiveness of, and compliance with, those regimes. Consistent with other policy priorities, we will also promote new agreements and arrangements that serve our nonproliferation goals. Overall, we seek to cultivate an international environment that is more conducive to nonproliferation. Our efforts will include:

Nuclear:

- Strengthening of the Nuclear Nonproliferation Treaty and International Atomic Energy Agency (IAEA), including through ratification of an IAEA Additional Protocol by all NPT states parties, assurances that all states put in place full-scope IAEA safeguards agreements, and appropriate increases in funding for the Agency;
- Negotiating a Fissile Material Cut-Off Treaty that advances U.S. security interests; and
- Strengthening the Nuclear Suppliers Group and Zangger Committee.

Chemical and Biological:

- Effective functioning of the Organization for the Prohibition of Chemical Weapons;
- Identification and promotion of constructive and realistic measures to strengthen the BWC and thereby to help meet the biological weapons threat; and
- Strengthening of the Australia Group.

Missile:

- Strengthening the Missile Technology Control Regime (MTCR), including through support for universal adherence to the International Code of Conduct Against Ballistic Missile Proliferation.

Nonproliferation and Threat Reduction Cooperation. The United States pursues a wide range of programs, including the Nunn-Lugar program, designed to address the proliferation threat stemming from the large quantities of Soviet-legacy WMD and missile-related expertise and materials. Maintaining an extensive and efficient set of nonproliferation and threat reduction assistance programs to Russia and other former Soviet states is a high priority. We will also continue to encourage friends and allies to increase their contributions to these programs, particularly through the G-8 Global Partnership Against the Spread of Weapons and Materials of Mass Destruction. In addition, we will work with other states to improve the security of their WMD-related materials.

Controls on Nuclear Materials. In addition to programs with former Soviet states to reduce fissile material and improve the security of that which remains, the United States will continue to discourage the worldwide accumulation of separated plutonium and to minimize the use of highly-enriched uranium. As outlined in the National Energy Policy, the United States will work in collaboration with international partners to develop recycle and fuel treatment technologies that are cleaner, more efficient, less waste-intensive, and more proliferation-resistant.

U.S. Export Controls. We must ensure that the implementation of U.S. export controls furthers our nonproliferation and other national security goals, while recognizing the realities that American businesses face in the increasingly globalized marketplace.

We will work to update and strengthen export controls using existing authorities. We also seek new legislation to improve the ability of our export control system to give full weight to both nonproliferation objectives and commercial interests. Our overall goal is to focus our resources on truly sensitive exports to hostile states or those that engage in onward proliferation, while removing unnecessary barriers in the global marketplace.

Nonproliferation Sanctions. Sanctions can be a valuable component of our overall strategy against WMD proliferation. At times, however, sanctions have proven inflexible and ineffective. We will develop a comprehensive sanctions policy to better integrate sanctions into our overall strategy and work with Congress to consolidate and modify existing sanctions legislation.

WMD consequence management

Defending the American homeland is the most basic responsibility of our government. As part of our defense, the United States must be fully prepared to respond to the consequences of WMD use on our soil, whether by hostile states or by terrorists. We must also be prepared to respond to the effects of WMD use against our forces deployed abroad, and to assist friends and allies.

The National Strategy for Homeland Security discusses U.S. Government programs to deal with the consequences of the use of a chemical, biological, radiological, or nuclear weapon in the United States. A number of these programs offer training, planning, and assistance to state and local governments. To maximize their effectiveness, these efforts need to be integrated and comprehensive. Our first responders must have the full range of protective, medical, and remediation tools to identify, assess, and respond rapidly to a WMD event on our territory.

The White House Office of Homeland Security will coordinate all federal efforts to prepare for and mitigate the consequences of terrorist attacks within the United States, including those involving WMD. The Office of Homeland Security will also work closely with state and local governments to ensure their planning, training, and equipment requirements are addressed. These issues, including the roles of the Department of Homeland Security, are addressed in detail in the National Strategy for Homeland Security.

The National Security Council's Office of Combating Terrorism coordinates and helps improve U.S. efforts to respond to and manage the recovery from terrorist attacks outside the United States. In cooperation with the Office of Combating Terrorism, the Department of State coordinates interagency efforts to work with our friends and allies to develop their own emergency preparedness and consequence management capabilities.

Integrating the pillars

Several critical enabling functions serve to integrate the three pillars—counterproliferation, nonproliferation, and consequence management—of the U.S. National Strategy to Combat WMD.

Improved Intelligence Collection and Analysis. A more accurate and complete understanding of the full range of WMD threats is, and will remain, among the highest U.S. intelligence priorities, to enable us to prevent proliferation, and to deter or defend against those who would use those capabilities against us. Improving our ability to obtain timely and accurate knowledge of adversaries' offensive and defensive capabilities, plans, and intentions is key to developing effective counter- and nonproliferation policies and capabilities. Particular emphasis must be accorded to improving: intelligence regarding WMD-related facilities and activities; interaction among U.S. intelligence, law enforcement, and military agencies; and intelligence cooperation with friends and allies.

Research and Development. The United States has a critical need for cutting-edge technology that can quickly and effectively detect, analyze, facilitate interdiction of, defend against, defeat, and mitigate the consequences of WMD. Numerous U.S. Government departments and agencies are currently engaged in the essential research and development to support our overall strategy against WMD proliferation.

The new Counterproliferation Technology Coordination Committee, consisting of senior representatives from all concerned agencies, will act to improve interagency coordination of U.S. Government counterproliferation research and development efforts. The Committee will assist in identifying priorities, gaps, and overlaps in existing programs and in examining options for future investment strategies.

Strengthened International Cooperation. WMD represent a threat not just to the United States, but also to our friends and allies and the broader international community. For this reason, it is vital that we work closely with like-minded countries on all elements of our comprehensive proliferation strategy.

A few states are dedicated proliferators, whose leaders are determined to develop, maintain, and improve their WMD and delivery capabilities.

Targeted Strategies Against Proliferants. All elements of the overall U.S. strategy to combat WMD must be brought to bear in targeted strategies against supplier and recipient states of WMD proliferation concern, as well as against terrorist groups which seek to acquire WMD.

A few states are dedicated proliferators, whose leaders are determined to develop, maintain, and improve their WMD and delivery capabilities, which directly threaten the United States, U.S. forces overseas, and/or our friends and allies. Because each of these regimes is different, we will pursue country-specific strategies that best enable us and our friends and allies to prevent, deter, and defend against WMD and missile threats from each of them. These strategies must also take into account the growing cooperation among proliferant states—so-called secondary proliferation— which challenges us to think in new ways about specific country strategies.

One of the most difficult challenges we face is to prevent, deter, and defend against the acquisition and use of WMD by terrorist groups. The current and potential future linkages between terrorist groups and state sponsors of terrorism are particularly dangerous and require priority attention. The full range of counterproliferation, nonproliferation, and consequence management measures must be brought to bear against the WMD terrorist threat, just as they are against states of greatest proliferation concern.

Our National Strategy to Combat WMD requires much of all of us—the Executive Branch, the Congress, state and local governments, the American people, and our friends and allies. The requirements to prevent, deter, defend against, and respond to today's WMD threats are complex and challenging. But they are not daunting. We can and will succeed in the tasks laid out in this strategy; we have no other choice.

2

Preemptive War Against Rogue Nations Is Necessary for National Security

Joshua Muravchik

Joshua Muravchik is the author of Exporting Democracy: Fulfilling America's Destiny *and* Heaven on Earth: The Rise and Fall of Socialism. *He is a resident scholar at the American Enterprise Institute, a public policy research organization.*

U.S. foreign policy has changed dramatically since September 11, 2001, and the most controversial new doctrine to emerge from these changes is the Bush administration's argument that the United States should preemptively attack rogue states that pose an immediate threat to the United States. The doctrine of preemption is justified because it is grounded in the right of national self-defense, which is the fundamental basis for international law. It is also justified because the doctrine is part of a broader effort to spread democracy in the Middle East. The major criticism of preemption is that the United States may use the doctrine to act unilaterally, without the explicit sanction of the United Nations, as it did in its invasion of Iraq in 2003. However, America is justified in pursuing morally sound foreign policies even in the face of United Nations opposition.

The "National Security Strategy of the United States" is a document that usually passes unnoticed. Commenting on the most ambitious one produced during the eight years of Bill Clinton's presidency, [political commentator] William Safire quipped that it "has been kept secret by the fiendishly clever device of making it public." In truth, these reports, which are supposed to be issued annually, and in the name of the President, are always made public and almost always ignored. Some of them have been written in the third person, suggesting that not even the document's putative author has read it.

It was thus a dramatic change when [in 2002], George W. Bush's first strategy statement provoked front-page headlines and incited a rash of greatly alarmed reactions at home and abroad. "Pugnacious," "arrogant," "sure to make the rest of the world uneasy," lamented the *New York Times*. "A call for . . . imperialism," protested Senator Edward Kennedy. "An implicit . . . denunciation of the modern state order," warned the columnist William Pfaff in the *International Herald Tribune*, who also likened the supposed revolutionary destructiveness of Bush's work to the *Communist Manifesto*.

What made this document so different from its predecessors was not only its content but its context. Earlier annual reports, the mandate for which had been enacted in 1986 just as the cold war was winding down, were usually empty exercises because, in the absence of a crystallized threat, "strategic planning" was itself hopelessly vague. But now, in the wake of the attacks of September 11, the President had proclaimed the nation to be at war with terrorism, and this document represented the fullest statement yet of his approach to that war.

We are not after any one state or group but have in our sights the entire global network of terrorists and their sponsors.

In this respect if in few others, the new strategy could be said to bear some resemblance to America's last grand strategy, "containment," which likewise developed more in practice than in abstraction. In the late 1940's, as Communists seized Poland and Czechoslovakia and grasped for Greece and Turkey, the United States came to realize that it faced a profound underlying danger. That danger was Soviet expansionism, and "containment" was our response to it. Similarly, George W. Bush concluded that the events of September 11 were but one terrible instance of a larger peril, and what he was now offering was a plan, however rough, for confronting it in its full dimension.

Indeed, it was Bush's insistence on this broad approach that aroused most of the controversy. Few Americans or Europeans may have doubted the need to combat terrorism or the organization called al Qaeda, and most proved willing to countenance our attack on al Qaeda's Taliban sponsors. But in speeches over the intervening months, Bush's invocation of an "axis of evil" [In his 2002 State of the Union address, Bush referred to the countries of Iran, Iraq, and North Korea as an "axis of evil."], his espousal of "regime change" in Iraq, his warning that each nation must choose which side it was on in the war against terror—all this had struck some Americans and most Europeans as too sweeping or too aggressive. Now, this ambitious plan for confronting a peril that according to Bush lay "at the crossroads of radicalism and technology" seemed to confirm their worst fears.

Three goals for U.S. national security

The strategy as presented articulates three goals: to "defend the peace by fighting terrorists and tyrants, . . . preserve the peace by building good relations among the great powers, . . . [and] extend the peace by encouraging free and open societies on every continent."

Explaining the first goal—why terrorists must be fought, and can no longer be viewed by us as a marginal phenomenon—the document asserts that whereas "enemies in the past needed great armies and great industrial capabilities to endanger America," today "shadowy networks of individuals can bring great chaos and suffering to our shores for less than it costs to purchase a single tank." While homeland defense is necessary, "our best defense is a good offense." This is the reason America is waging "war against terrorists of global reach."

Since the terrorists' "shadowy networks" batten on support from governments, the document also repeats more than once Bush's earlier insistence that "we make no distinction between terrorists and those who knowingly harbor or provide aid to them." Among the now familiar checklist of tools that can be used against terrorism, including "law enforcement, intelligence, and vigorous efforts to cut off terrorist financing," it lays stress on two: "wag[ing] a war of ideas" and military force. The latter embraces, pointedly, the "exercise [of] our right of self-defense by acting preemptively against . . . terrorists, to prevent them from doing harm against our people and our country." Ideally such action will be taken in concert with partners, but "we will not hesitate to act alone, if necessary."

Dire though the terrorist threat is, it does not rise to the level of the threat once posed by the Soviet Union. The President's second stated goal—preserving the peace—aims at averting a recurrence of precisely that kind of danger. "Today," the report asserts, "the international community has the best chance since the rise of the nation-state in the 17th century to build a world where great powers compete in peace instead of continually prepare for war." Of course, such ideals have often been voiced before, ordinarily as a vision of the distant day when lions will lie down with lambs. Bush, however, treats this as a practical goal, thereby giving the first glimpse of the unlikely radicalism of his whole approach.

The complaint that Bush's doctrine of preemption traduces international law is the most serious charge laid against it. But is it well founded?

To fulfill this vision, Bush proposes to work toward ever more friendly relations with Russia and China. As against those who believe that China is likely to emerge as a key American rival, the document states that "We welcome the emergence of a strong, peaceful, and prosperous China." At the same time, it affirms the need for China to democratize, and proclaims "our commitment to the self-defense of Taiwan."

But the goal of preserving a world without great-power conflict also entails a harder edge: namely, maintaining America's military supremacy. Bush's statement vows that "our forces will be strong enough to dissuade potential adversaries from pursuing a military build-up in hopes of surpassing, or equaling, the power of the United States."

In expounding the third goal of Bush's strategy—extending the peace—the statement draws from the experience of the 20th century the lesson that there is only "a single sustainable model for national success: freedom, democracy, and free enterprise." Accordingly, Bush promises to "make freedom and the development of democratic institutions key themes in our bilateral relations" and to "speak out honestly about violations of the nonnegotiable demands of human dignity." Toward that end he proposes a 50-percent increase in U.S. "core development assistance"— that is, foreign aid—directed to "countries whose governments rule justly, invest in their people, and encourage economic freedom."

The document also contains the usual potpourri of pledges: to modernize our military, promote free trade, and defuse regional conflicts. But the essence of the strategy lies in the three goals I have described, and it is these that have been the focus of controversy. Or rather the first two have drawn attack, while the third, which constitutes the most important and most ambitious component of the strategy, has been relatively ignored.

Specious objections to preemptive war

The most intense controversy has surrounded the issue of preemptive war. In the statement itself, Bush's defense of the legitimacy of preemption serves to buttress the case for going to war specifically to oust Saddam Hussein. But as former Vice President Al Gore pointed out in a much publicized rejoinder to the document, "the existing [UN] resolutions from 1991 are sufficient from a legal standpoint" to justify resuming hostilities with Iraq. Why, then, did Bush grasp this hot potato?

Probably the answer is that he wanted to lay out something more than a narrow legal argument for going to war. He wanted an argument that appealed, as he put it, to "common sense." It was not only Saddam Hussein's violation of UN Security Council resolutions that justified the risks and costs of war; it was the terrifying danger he would pose if armed with nuclear weapons. In addition, the President may have wanted to underline the earnestness of his own repeated assertions that we are not after any one state or group but rather have in our sights the entire global network of terrorists and their sponsors.

Three main objections have been raised to Bush's doctrine of preemption in this larger context. The first is that it is open-ended. If the United States claims the right to attack Iraq today, whom will it turn on tomorrow? Bush's strategy, reported *Time*, "argues that the strongest nation in the world has the right to preemptively attack anyone who seeks to harm its people or interests."

With the UN having failed to develop into a genuine rampart of peace and security, the preexisting right of states to provide their own security [remains] intact.

The second objection, less jaundiced in its view of American aims, concentrates not so much on the temptation to inaugurate wars hither and yon as on the precedent we may be establishing for others—a precedent only too open to exploitation by less scrupulous states. Thus, a

Brookings Institution analysis raised the troubling prospect that "other countries will embrace the preemption argument as a cover for settling their own national-security scores."

The third objection is that the policy of preemption will shred the fabric of international law. "What this doctrine does," said Gore, "is to destroy the goal of a world in which states consider themselves subject to law."

Preemptive attacks limited to terrorists and rogue states

All three objections are debatable, if not downright specious. The first simply misrepresents the statement. Contrary to *Time*, and contrary to Gore's plaint that Bush has arrogated to himself: the "right to preemptively attack whomsoever he may deem represents a potential future threat," the document makes plain that the policy of preemption is aimed at terrorists and "rogue states" alone. The latter term, coined in the Clinton administration, is here given precise definition perhaps for the first time.

Rogue states, says the strategy paper, have a number of identifiable characteristics. They

> brutalize their own people and squander their national resources for the personal gain of the rulers; display no regard for international law, threaten their neighbors, and callously violate international treaties to which they are party; are determined to acquire weapons of mass destruction, along with other advanced military technology, to be used as threats or offensively to achieve their aggressive designs; sponsor terrorism around the globe; and reject basic human values and hate the United States and everything for which it stands.

This is a definition that would readily apply to the three members of Bush's "axis of evil," and perhaps to Muammar Qaddafi's Libya—but to few, if any, others. One might challenge aspects of the enumerated criteria, but the claim that Bush has sought an unlimited writ for preemptive action is nonsense.

More reasonable is the fear that others might borrow the doctrine of preemption for their own, less savory purposes. Some states, no doubt, will try to do precisely that. But (to anticipate somewhat the third objection) there is less cause for alarm here than meets the eye, for the fear rests on the assumption that international law acts as a substantial barrier to misbehavior by states. In truth, international law is not self-enforcing, and serves as a barrier only insofar as states, meaning usually the United States, are willing to enforce it. In practice, miscreant nations routinely cloak their actions in spurious claims of self-defense or of other rights enshrined in law. It is not the cleverness of their arguments but rather the willingness of others to bear the burdens of counteracting them that determines what they will get away with.

To say, however, that international law is not self-enforcing and that its enforcement depends largely on the United States is not to say that international law is of no value to the United States. On the contrary, if all nations lived up to the law, the achievement of America's major international objectives—peace, human rights, fair commerce—would be assured. Since many do not live up to it, our success depends on our own power. But the law affords us a recognized and objective standard for exercising that power. Granted, it may present a constraint on our freedom of action, but that is a price worth paying for the legitimacy it confers on the most important objectives of our policy.

For this reason, the complaint that Bush's doctrine of preemption traduces international law is the most serious charge laid against it. But is it well founded? Bush's statement does not strike a posture that places America above the law, as some critics have suggested. To the contrary, it seeks to embed the new doctrine in established legal traditions. "For centuries," it asserts, "international law [has] recognized that nations need not suffer an attack before they can lawfully take action to defend themselves." And it continues: "We must adapt [this] concept of imminent threat to the capabilities and objectives of today's adversaries." Those capabilities include weapons of mass destruction that can be "easily concealed, delivered covertly, and used without warning."

The right of self-defense

In this, Bush is on strong legal ground. The issue of preemption is as old as international law itself. Hugo Grotius, the 17th-century Dutch political philosopher who first formulated the idea of international law, asserted the legality of "kill[ing] him who is preparing to kill." Emmerich de Vattel, the second most important name in the early development of international law, explained further:

> A nation has the right to resist the injury that another seeks to inflict upon it, and to use force . . . against the aggressor. It may even anticipate the other's design, being careful, however, not to act upon vague and doubtful suspicions, lest it should run the risk of becoming itself the aggressor.

The right of self-defense was asserted by the U.S. government in the course of the negotiation of the Kellogg-Briand Pact of 1928 [an agreement among sixty-two nations to renounce war as an instrument of national policy] in such absolute terms as to encompass preemptive self-defense as well. The State Department then declared:

> The right to self-defense . . . is inherent in every sovereign state and implicit in every treaty. Every nation is free at all times and regardless of treaty provisions to defend its territory from attack or invasion and it alone is competent to decide whether circumstances require recourse to war in self-defense.

As the State Department also acknowledged, such a broad understanding might well mean that what one state would claim as self-defense would be called aggression by another. There was no solution to this, it said, except that the state whose claim was well-founded would be accorded the general sympathy of the rest of the world.

The United Nations was created in order to move the world beyond a situation in which victims had no recourse but "self-help" to one in which all states could rely upon a global structure of peace. This would be made up of the rules and procedures enumerated in chapter seven of the UN Charter, whose enforcement is the principal responsibility of the Security Council. But it was hardly expected that states would simultaneously give up their prior rights. As the relevant sentence reads: "Nothing in the present charter shall impair the inherent right of individual or collective self-defense if an armed attack occurs against a member of the United Nations, until the Security Council has taken the measures necessary to maintain international peace and security."

Beyond the urgencies of self-defense, Bush aims to neutralize the threats we face by spreading the balm of democracy.

True, this wording left some mystery as to whether the "inherent right" of self-defense would be "impaired" in cases other than when an armed attack had already taken place, such as in the face of a threat of attack. Perhaps the clearest test of this very issue occurred in 1967, when the Arab states sought a Security Council condemnation of Israel's preemptive strikes that inaugurated the Six-Day war. The Security Council rebuffed the Arab motion, and so did the General Assembly. . . . In other words, the UN did not judge Israel's first strike to have been illegal.

Legal niceties aside, common sense likewise tells us that the right of self-defense cannot be compromised by the adoption of the UN Charter, if only because chapter seven has, in sad reality, proved to be a dead letter. It envisions a UN general staff and a commitment of substantial military resources by all member states to a mighty international force, to be deployed as needed by the Security Council in order to enforce the peace. In practice, the UN has managed to fulfill this role exactly twice in its history: in Korea in 1950 and in the Persian Gulf in 1991. Both were unusual moments of Security Council comity not readily replicated (in the former case, the U.S. was able to take advantage of the fact that the Soviet delegate was boycotting the session). And in both cases, the assembled military forces, although they flew a UN flag, were largely American. With the UN having failed to develop into a genuine rampart of peace and security, the preexisting right of states to provide their own security must be assumed to remain intact.

Preempting the use of weapons of mass destruction

If the right to self-defense, including anticipatory self-defense, remains above dispute, that still leaves open the question of whether this principle may be extended, as in Bush's interpretation, to cover the right to take action against the deployment or imminent deployment of weapons of mass destruction in an aggressive manner or by an aggressive state. Citing this very case, some have said that the Bush strategy strays beyond the issue of preemption, where the threat is immediate and palpable, to claim a new right of preventive war. But the distinction between the two concepts is not so easy to make. The reasons were spelled out by President John F. Kennedy in response to the appearance of Soviet missiles in Cuba in 1962: "We no longer live," said Kennedy,

> in a world where only the actual firing of weapons represents a sufficient challenge to a nation's security to constitute maximum peril. Nuclear weapons are so destructive and ballistic missiles are so swift that any substantially increased possibility of their use or any sudden change in their deployment may well be regarded as a definite threat to peace.

Similar reasoning informed Israel's decision to bomb Iraq's nuclear plant at Osirak in 1981. As it happens, that action was condemned by the Security Council (by then, the UN's anti-Israel majority had strengthened), and the United States joined in the vote. In retrospect, however, a number of U.S. officials have publicly regretted this stance, and it is doubtful that, were the events rerun, the U.S. would act today as it did in 1981. As Secretary of State Colin Powell said recently: "It was a clear preemptive military strike. Everyone now is quite pleased [that Israel did it] even though they got the devil criticized out of them at the time."

What this suggests is that, as with most questions of international law, there is no definitive answer to the legal soundness of Bush's doctrine of preemption in cases involving weapons of mass destruction. But there can be no doubt whatsoever that powerful legal arguments exist on its behalf. The politicians and pundits who decry it as a travesty of international law are talking through their hats. . . .

U.S. unilateralism

This brings us to the final complaint about the strategy paper, which is that it embodies the already much-decried Bush tendency toward "unilateralism." "If the unilateralists [in Washington] get their way," said former Mexican president Ernesto Zedillo, who now writes a column for *Forbes*, "bin Laden . . . will have won." For his part, Al Gore fretted that Bush was sabotaging "America's prospects for continuing the historic leadership we began providing" when we persuaded the world to found the United Nations.

One would never know from these comments that Bush's paper makes a deep bow to multilateralism, affirming that "there is little of lasting consequence that the United States can accomplish in the world without the sustained cooperation of its allies and friends in Canada and Europe." But the real point has to do with the pious invocation of multilateralism itself as a self-evidently noble thing. In World War II, the Axis powers were a multilateral force, while for a time Britain fought unilaterally. The Czechoslovaks stood alone in 1968, as the multilateral forces of the Warsaw Pact snuffed out their hopes for freedom. Israel fought alone in 1948 as the multilateral forces of the Arab League tried to strangle it in its cradle. In short, the moral standing of multilateral action depends entirely on circumstances and aims.

Much of the criticism of the Bush administration's unilateralism has centered on its rejection of such initiatives as the Kyoto Protocol on global warming, the International Criminal Court, and the like. But a nation's obligation under international law is to obey the law that exists, not to join in creating new law that it finds ill-considered. Bush makes this point obliquely in the strategy paper when he says that "international obligations are to be taken seriously . . . not to be undertaken symbolically." In any case, though, what rankles critics of American unilateralism even more than our reluctance to adopt specific initiatives is the unwillingness of the United States to subordinate itself in general to the United Nations. Here they are being hypocritical.

Critics [of U.S. foreign policy] offer no real alternative strategy, only a counsel of evasion.

To repeat: in its main political purposes, the United Nations has been an almost wholly feckless body throughout its 57 years, except for those rare occasions on which it has in effect subordinated itself to U.S. policy. It is difficult to imagine any other nation engaging in the kind of self-abnegation that has been demanded of the United States vis-a-vis the UN, least of all some of the nations most critical of American unilateralism. There is in fact ample reason to believe that this demand is itself motivated by nothing more than national egoism on the part of states that envy America's power or see themselves as rivals. As Fareed Zakaria has put it: "France and Russia have turned the United Nations into a stage from which to pursue naked self-interest. They have used multilateralism as a way to further unilateral policies." Nor would such American truckling do anything but harm to the causes of peace and human rights, causes that are upheld more consistently by the United States than by the United Nations.

A Wilsonian approach to U.S. foreign policy

More important than whether the United States acts unilaterally or multilaterally are the purposes for which it acts. And here we come to the most interesting and important, not to say astonishing, aspects of the Bush strategy, if also the ones that have been the most overlooked. For these add up to nothing less than the resurrection of a Wilsonian approach to U.S. foreign policy.

The term *Wilsonian* is sometimes used to suggest an obtuse utopianism. But in its best construction it connotes both a sensitivity to moral considerations and an enlightened self-interest that links our own well-being to the state of the world around us.

However much the new national-security strategy may contemplate unilateral action, its aims are to promote the general good. "We do not use our strength to press for unilateral advantage," the document declares. "We seek instead to create a balance of power that favors human freedom." And it adds: "the aim of this strategy is to help make the world not just safer but better."

Those who are suspicious of American motives will dismiss these pronouncements as self-serving. But they are a very far cry from the words of George Bush during the 2000 election campaign. When asked, "Have you formed any guiding principles for exercising [America's] enormous power?," the Republican presidential candidate replied: "The first question is what's in the best interests of the United States."

If its concern for the general good is one sense in which Bush's strategy may be called Wilsonian, another is its insistence that America's ideals must constitute the starting point for America's policies. On this point, the document states:

> In pursuit of our goals, our first imperative is to clarify what we stand for: the United States must defend liberty and justice because these principles are right and true for all people everywhere. No nation owns these aspirations, and no nation is exempt from them.

Furthermore, Bush is convinced that American principles are of universal validity, and his strategy statement contains as forceful an assertion of this universalism as may be found:

> People everywhere want to be able to speak freely; choose who will govern them; worship as they please; educate their children—male and female; own property; and enjoy the benefits of their labor. These values of freedom are right and true for every person, in every society—and the duty of protecting these values against their enemies is the common calling of freedom-loving people across the globe and across the ages.

Then there is the choice of methods for a long-term solution to the problems addressed by this strategy. Fighting terrorists and maintaining our military superiority are essential to our safety in the here and now; but beyond the urgencies of self-defense, Bush aims to neutralize the threats we face by spreading the balm of democracy. What, after all, is a "balance of power that favors human freedom" but an echo of the slogan under which Woodrow Wilson led America into World War I?

A few commentators have in fact picked up on this Wilsonian spirit in Bush's national-security strategy. The one who has captured it most cogently and sympathetically is the historian John Lewis Gaddis, writing in *Foreign Policy*. For Gaddis,

> There is a compellingly realistic reason now to complete the idealistic task Woodrow Wilson began more than eight decades age: the world must be made safe for democracy, because otherwise democracy will not be safe in the world. The Bush . . . report could be, therefore, the most important reformulation of U.S. grand strategy in over half a century. . . .

Courage to confront the problems in the Middle East

President Bush has also faced squarely, as did none of his predecessors, the deep political sickness in the greater Middle East out of which grew the specific danger that manifested itself on September 11. On the scale developed by Freedom House, on which 1 means most free and 7 means least free, the median score of the 22 Arab states is 5.5, while the median for all the world's other nations is 2.5. (Iran, not Arab but a part of the same political culture, scores a miserable 6.) The UN's own Arab Human Development Report, itself compiled by a team of Arab intellectuals, concludes that this region suffers from critical deficits of freedom, women's empowerment, and "human capabilities and knowledge relative to income." Although the Arab world is far richer than sub-Saharan Africa, it scored appreciably worse on the UN report's measures of freedom and other social goods.

What all of these barometers mean, in less euphemistic terms, is that this is a region characterized by paranoia, apocalypticism, tyranny, and violence, a region where differences are settled by the sword. Societies that behave this way internally can hardly be relied upon to settle issues with the outside pacifically.

Bush's predecessors accepted the political culture of the Middle East as a given to which America had to adapt. Clinton hosted Yasir Arafat more often than any other foreign leader; Bush senior was especially close to the Saudis; Ronald Reagan traded arms for hostages with Iran; and Jimmy Carter paid fawning visits to the Syrian dictator Hafez al-Assad. But September 11 seems to have convinced George W. Bush that another approach is needed. Although he has taken every occasion to stress that our enemy is not Islam, he has decided nonetheless to try to transform the Middle East. . . .

Military conquest, perhaps surprisingly to some, has often proved to be an effective means of implanting democracy. Nevertheless, the United States is hardly about to invade countries that pose no military threat solely for the purpose of democratizing them. There are, however, political measures by means of which the project of democratization can be advanced elsewhere in the Middle East. Some have already been initiated by the Bush administration; others will have to be adopted if the strategy is to succeed. These include: continuing to insist on openness and accountability in the Palestinian Authority, safeguarding Afghanistan's political and economic reconstruction, supporting the political liberalization under way in Qatar and Bahrain, rethinking our blank-check policy toward the domestic behavior of Egypt and Saudi Arabia, championing the independence of Lebanon, and working to undermine the retrograde regimes of Syria and Libya. . . .

Courage to lead

But words are one thing, acts another. Having devised and presented a strategy apposite to the threat confronting the United States, George Bush must demonstrate the skill, courage, and determination to execute it. And there will be obstacles aplenty, not least from the critics whose ranks multiply with every sign of presidential wavering and whose warnings and plaints sound uncannily like those faced in an earlier age by Harry S. Truman when he launched the policy of containment.

Truman's request for aid to Greece and Turkey was denounced by one prominent Senator as "a new American imperialism," aimed at securing "oil for the American monopolies." The columnist Walter Lippmann warned that by failing to work through the newly established UN, Truman had "cut a hole in the charter which it would be very difficult to repair." It was only because such voices were spurned that the world was eventually delivered from the shadow of Soviet tyranny.

Now as then, the critics offer no real alternative strategy, only a counsel of evasion. In 1947, when the UN was but two years old, the notion that the world body could serve as a substitute for the exercise of America's own will and power may perhaps have been a pardonable hope. Today, when we "know better, such advice is worse than pusillanimous; it is utterly cynical. By contrast, Bush's response to the challenge that was brought home to us last September 11 is both thoughtful and brave. Our national security is indeed at issue. Everything now is riding on the follow-through.

3

The U.S. Doctrine of Preemptive War Is Misguided

Charles W. Kegley Jr. and Gregory A. Raymond

Charles W. Kegley Jr. is an associate editor of USA Today, *a professor of international relations at the University of South Carolina, and the author of* American Foreign Policy: Pattern and Process. *Gregory A. Raymond is director of the Honors College of Boise (Idaho) State University and the author of* Conflict Resolution and the Structure of the State System.

Throughout history, the aggressors in most wars have justified their belligerence by arguing that one must act preemptively to prevent enemies from attacking. Following the same line of reasoning, the Bush administration has strongly argued for the need to strike preemptively against rogue states that threaten the United States. However, if the United States embraces a doctrine of preemptive war, other nations are likely to follow suit. U.S. security may be enhanced in the short term, but in the long term, global stability will be diminished and the possibility of war will increase.

In the immediate aftermath of the terrorist attacks on Sept. 11, 2001, the U.S. began a war against global terrorism. Soon thereafter, America abandoned its Cold War strategy of containment [whose goal was to prevent the spread of communism from the Soviet bloc], embracing the doctrine of preemptive warfare aimed at attacking suspected aggressors before they could strike first. This, in turn, led to the invasion of Iraq in March, 2003.

The Bush Administration's doctrine of preempting terrorists and rogue states, in what is called alternatively "forward deterrence" or "anticipatory self-defense," raises anew timeless moral and legal issues about the conditions under which, and purposes for which, a just war for self-defense is permissible to counter a threat to national security. What it has advanced as a new national security strategy is nothing less than an amputation of the normative pillar on which global society has been based at least since 1928, when the Kellogg-Briand pact outlawed war as an in-

Charles W. Kegley Jr. and Gregory A. Raymond, "Preemptive War: A Prelude to Global Peril," *USA Today*, vol. 131, May 2003, p. 14. Copyright © 2003 by Society for the Advancement of Education. Reproduced by permission.

strument of foreign policy. This radical revision of customary international law is leading the world into uncharted waters. If it becomes permissible to attack other international actors who do not pose an *imminent* threat, then, without a moral principle to guide international conduct, war is likely to increase.

Origins of the Bush doctrine

President Bush first signaled the policy change he was initiating on June 1, 2002, at West Point. To his way of thinking, 9/11 created unprecedented "new deadly challenges" that necessitated new approaches and rules for statecraft. Chastising tyrants like Iraq's Saddam Hussein as international outlaws, the President announced that "We must be prepared to stop rogue states and their terrorist clients before they are able to threaten or use weapons of mass destruction against the United States and our allies and friends. . . . Traditional concepts of deterrence will not work against a terrorist enemy whose avowed tactics are wanton destruction and the targeting of innocents, whose so-called soldiers seek martyrdom in death. . . . The greater the threat, the greater the risk of inaction—and the more compelling the case for taking anticipatory action to defend ourselves, even if uncertainty remains as to the time and place of the enemy's attack. To forestall or *prevent* such hostile acts by our adversaries, the United States will, if necessary, act preemptively." (Emphasis added.)

This reasoning soon thereafter became the cornerstone of *The National Security Strategy of the United States of America* (NSS), released on Sept. 17 [2002]. It reiterated Bush's West Point declaration that the era of deterrence was over and preemption was an idea whose time had come. It then proceeded to assert that, "Given the goals of rogue states and terrorists, the United States can no longer solely rely on a reactive posture as we have in the past. . . . We cannot let our enemies strike first." The NSS added, "Nations need not suffer an attack before they can lawfully take action to defend themselves against forces that present an imminent danger of attack."

If it becomes permissible to attack other international actors who do not pose an imminent *threat, . . . war is likely to increase.*

The extreme revisionism of the Bush doctrine undercuts a key preemptory norm in international law that underpins all others—the use of force cannot be justified merely on account of an adversary's capabilities, but solely in defense against its aggressive actions. Preemption represents a frontal rejection of Articles 2(4) and 51 of the United Nations Charter that condones war only in self-defense. It opens the door to military first strikes against adversaries, under the claim that their motives are evil and that they are building the military capabilities to inflict mass destruction.

It is not difficult to appreciate the grave dangers that have prompted this watershed in U.S. national strategy. The threats which provoked the President's extreme strategic response are real. *Raison d'etat* dictates that actions be taken for the preservation of the state, and, in these threatening circumstances, many find reasonable the claim that the national interest makes such countermeasures imperative. The temptation to attack first an adversary who might attack you is, of course, often overwhelming. Why stand by in the face of a potential threat? "An ounce of prevention is worth a pound of cure," a popular cliche advises. Better to hit an enemy before it attacks, than to be left prostrate. The thinking underlying the rationale is expressed well in Umberto Eco's *Baudolino*, where the protagonist argues, "Better to be rid at once of someone who does not yet threaten you, than leave him alive so that he may threaten you one day. Let us strike first."

That realpolitik logic was at the root of the NSS proposition that the "best defense is a good offense," and the premise behind the President's explanation in an Oct. 7, 2002, speech in Cincinnati that "We have every reason to assume the worst, and we have an urgent duty to prevent the worst from happening." A proactive policy through preemption is defined as necessary because it was argued that America "cannot wait for the final proof—the smoking gun—that could come in the form of a mushroom cloud."

[The historical] record suggests that preventive war is a problem, not a solution.

Fear is a great motivator. There are ample reasons to fear terrorists like Osama bin Laden and tyrants like Saddam. The threats are real in this age of globalization in which boundaries are no longer barriers to external threats, a suitcase nuclear bomb or a chemical/biological weapon can obliterate any American city, and a terrorist can strike anywhere and anytime. The U.S. *is* vulnerable, so there is an understandable compulsion to eliminate threats by any means available, including preemptive strikes.

Preemption is advocated as a policy, but what must be understood is that this strategy goes beyond that goal to a whole other level—to *preventive* war. The Bush doctrine transcends the established limitations of the use of armed force in self-defense against a prior armed attack. "The President is not 'reserving a right' to respond to imminent threats," wrote Duke University professor of international relations Michael Byers in the July 25, 2002, issue of *The London Review of Books*, "he is seeking an extension of the fight of self-defense to include action against potential future dangers."

As the wording of the Bush NSS illuminates, the line between preemption and prevention is blurry. How does one distinguish intentions from capabilities? Because an adversary amasses arsenals of weapons, does that necessarily mean that those weapons are for aggression instead of defense? Without knowledge of motives, prudence dictates worst-case assumptions. This invites the so-called "security dilemma" that results when one country's arms acquisitions provokes corresponding actions by alarmed adversaries, with the result that all participants in the arms race experience reduced security as their weaponry increases. Preemption addresses the danger by attacking first and asking questions about intentions later.

Preemptive strikes throughout history

The quest to redefine international rules to permit preemptive strikes has deeper philosophical, ethical, and legal consequences for the long term, beyond its unforeseen immediate impact. Does it threaten to weaken international security and, paradoxically, U.S. national security as well? To probe this question, let us look briefly at some historical precedents to preemptive practices in order to put the current policy into perspective. Consider some salient illustrations that precede Bush's rationale:

• In the third Punic War fought between the Roman and Carthaginian empires (264–147 B.C.), after a 50-year hiatus, the Romans bought the advice of the 81-year-old Cato the Elder. Consumed with the fear that renewed Punic power would culminate eventually in Roman defeat unless drastic military measures were taken, he ended every speech to the Roman Senate by proclaiming *"Carthaginian esse delendum"* (Carthage must be destroyed). Heeding Cato's advice, Rome launched a preventive war of annihilation and, in 146 B.C., some 500,000 Carthaginian citizens were destroyed in an act of mass genocide, and an entire civilization was obliterated. The foreign threat *had* been met; thereafter, no challenges to Roman hegemony existed—but at what cost? The Roman historian Polybius prophetically lamented, "I feel a terror and dread lest someone someday should give the same order about my own native city." Perhaps this led him to conclude that "it is not the object of war to annihilate those who have given provocation to it, but to cause them to mend their ways." Worse still, this preventive war can be said to have destroyed the soul of Rome. After it, Rome suffered a prolonged period of revolutionary strife, and much later found itself victim of the same savage preemptive measures by invaders it had once inflicted on Carthage. *"Val victis"* (Woe betide the defeated), the Romans cried after the city was sacked by the Gauls in 390 A.D. Is there an object lesson here? Read on.

• Dec. 7, 1941, was "a day that will live in infamy," as Pres. Franklin D. Roosevelt declared in reaction to Japan's sneak attack on Pearl Harbor. That strike removed most of the U.S. Pacific fleet and thereby redressed the Japanese-American military balance of power. The attack was premeditated, for arguably preventive purposes—to hit the U.S. before it could use its superior military capabilities to smother Japanese imperialism and Japan's Asian Co-Prosperity Sphere in its cradle. However, preventive action hardly proved practical. It backfired, provoking the sleeping American giant from isolationistic neutrality into an angry wrath without restraint, leading to the annihilating atomic bombing of Hiroshima on Aug. 6, 1945.

• In June, 1981, Iraq was making rapid headway, with French assistance, toward building a nuclear reactor. Israeli warplanes destroyed that facility in a strike that prevented Iraq from acquiring nuclear weapons. The attack was planned, and, with pinpoint accuracy and effectiveness, the potential threat (that Prime Minister Menachem Begin regarded as the most-serious challenge to Israeli self-preservation) was removed. Begin, a former terrorist, undertook terrorism against a proven terrorist and tyrant, thus practicing the same strategy he sought to contain. As G. John Ikenberry, the Peter F. Krogh Professor of Geopolitics and Global Justice at Georgetown University, notes, this attack broke normative barriers, "and the world condemned it as an act of aggression"—as unjustifiable and shortsighted. The Reagan Administration condemned the strike; France pronounced it "unacceptable"; and Great Britain berated it as "a grave breach of international law." The strategy worked, however, in the short run, as Iraqi plans for cross-border attacks on Kuwait, Iran, and, in all likelihood, Israel were averted. In the long run, though, the preventive attack strengthened Saddam's grip on power at home and animated his military ambitions to try harder—in the name of defense.

History is thus replete with examples of states that have rationalized preemptive surgical attacks against a rival for preventive purposes. In fact, it is hard to find many cases of states that did not claim that, in initiating war, they were merely acting prudently in self-defense. Nearly all wars have been justified by that claim. This record suggests that preventive war is a problem, not a solution.

What is likely to result if global norms are redefined to permit all states to defend themselves against potential threats . . . before an enemy undertakes an attack?

Bush asserts that, "If we wait for threats to fully materialize, we will have waited too long." That justification has been voiced by many before as an excuse for war. As *New York Times* columnist Bill Keller observes, historians cite as U.S. examples of preemptive interventions "Woodrow Wilson's occupation of Haiti in 1915, Lyndon Johnson's dispatch of U.S. Marines to the Dominican Republic in 1965, and Ronald Reagan's invasion of Grenada in 1983. [But] while preemption has been an occasional fact of life, [until George W. Bush] no president has so explicitly elevated the practice to a doctrine. Previous American leaders preferred to fabricate pretexts [such as] the sinking of the *Maine* . . . rather than admit they were going in 'unprovoked.'"

If a permissive climate of opinion on the acceptability of preemptive and preventive warfare takes root, will the U.S. and the world at large be safer and more secure? The normative barriers to the first-strike initiation of war vanish in a world in which preemption for prevention is accepted. Let us examine the blaring downside of the U.S. advocacy of preemptive warfare.

What if every nation embraced preemption?

Preemption and its extension to preventive war is a direct challenge to prevailing norms. To encapsulate the international legal consensus prior to 9/11, before U.S. doctrine began to challenge it, one might say that international law over time had gravitated toward increasingly restrictive sets of rules for justified war making. Aggressive war was illegal, but defensive war was not. International law, therefore, did not break down whenever war broke out, for there are specified conditions under which states were permitted to wage a war. Those criteria were highly restrictive, though, confining war to serve as a penal method for punishing a prior attack by an aggressor.

How the U.S. chooses to act—its code of conduct—will be a powerful determinant of the rules followed throughout the international arena. Global leaders lead in creating the system's rules. When the reigning hegemon abandons an established rule and endorses a substitute one, the rules change for everyone. What the strongest do eventually defines what everybody should do, and when a practice becomes common it tends to be seen as obligatory. As Harvard University professor of international relations Stanley Hoffmann puts it, rules *of* behavior become rules *for* behavior.

Changing circumstances call for changes in policy, and extreme times of trouble invite extreme responses. However, policies engineered in crises have rarely proven wise. In judging the ethics of a proposed standard of action, it is enlightening to recall German philosopher Immanuel Kant's insight into the situation. In his famous principle, the "categorical imperative," Kant asked humanity to consider, when contemplating an action or a policy, what the consequences would be if everyone practiced that same conduct. In evaluating the probity and prudential value of an action, he counseled that the sole ethical international activity is one that would be advantageous for humanity if it were to become a universal law practiced by all. Would that activity make for a better world? If all behave accordingly, as the practice becomes customary, would humanity benefit or suffer?

Kant preached an ethic that springs from the question "What if everybody did that?" and applied it to international relations. He believed, that the best reason for abiding by the ethics of Jesus Christ as propounded in the Sermon on the Mount was that those nonviolent principles would make for a better, more-rewarding life for all, and that killing creates a hell on Earth. We should treat others as we ourselves would wish to be treated, because those actions will, reciprocally, provoke others to treat us as we treat them. Nonaggression thus serves not only our best ideals, but benefits our self-interest, as reciprocity in altruism creates better relationships and a better world in which to live. This is the realism of idealism.

"If everyone embraces [the doctrine of preemption], a messy world would become a lot messier."

Taking this a short step forward, other questions can be asked about the moral responsibilities of the strong and mighty. What are the obligations of the powerful? How should they react to threats from weaker states? In asymmetrical contests of will, where the playing field is strongly slanted to the advantage of a superpower such as the U.S., should it play according to the same rules as its enemies? Lowering itself to the modus operandi of the likes of Saddam can reduce the U.S. superpower to the standards of those it opposes. Flexing military muscles without an international mandate and without convincing justification can prostitute traditional and honorable American principles, erode the U.S.'s reputation, and undermine its capacity to lead. To practice what is not right is to sacrifice respect for a country's most-valuable asset—its reputation for virtue, the most-important factor in what is known as "soft power" in the exercise of global influence.

Can smashing perceived threats serve justice efficiently? Recall moral philosopher John Rawls' simple test of justice—"Would the best off accept the arrangements if they believed at any moment they might find themselves in the same place of the worst off?" Historian Christopher Dawson provided a partial answer when he noted that, "As soon as men decide that all means are permitted to fight an evil, then their good becomes indistinguishable from the evil they set out to destroy."

Applying this reasoning, what is likely to result if global norms are redefined to permit all states to defend themselves against potential threats in advance, before an enemy undertakes an attack or inflicts an injury? What if the U.S. doctrine becomes every state's and every terrorist movement's policy?

What the big powers do sets the standards that others follow. If other states act on the same rationale the U.S. has promulgated and take preventive military action against any enemy they claim is threatening them, the right to use force will be legitimized. The danger is that every country could conclude that preemption for preventive purposes is an acceptable practice. This doctrine of preemption would invite any state to attack any adversary that it perceived was threatening it.

A bottomless legal pit

Perhaps unwittingly, the Bush Administration appears not to have taken into consideration the probability that its doctrine will encourage most others to accept that same doctrine, or that a bottomless legal pit will be created. "The specific doctrine of preemptive action," argues Ikenberry, "poses a problem: once the United States feels it can take such a course of action, nothing will stop other countries from doing the same." Indeed, that prophecy has already been fulfilled as others have emulated the American position by taking "up preemption as a way of dealing with these problems. The Bush doctrine—or at best the rhetoric—has already been appropriated by Russia against Georgia, by India against Pakistan. The dominoes can be expected to fall if the strategy of preemption continues to spread, as surely it will if the United States pursues its new policy." Or, as Keller opines, "If everyone embraces [the U.S.] new doctrine, a messy world would become a lot messier. Caveat pre-emptor."

If a permissive climate of opinion on the acceptability of preemptive and preventive warfare takes root, will the U.S. and the world at large be safer and more secure? That is doubtful. It has taken a long time for an international consensus to build behind the view that a preemptive attack to prevent an enemy's potential attack is outside the boundaries of justified warfare. In earlier epochs, states believed that they could attack another country for any reason deemed in the attacker's national interests. That climate of normative opinion has evaporated, and, partially as a consequence, the frequency of interstate war has steadily declined and almost vanished since the Cold War ended. Now, however, the U.S. has justified preemptive war under the claim that the benefits of preemption exceed the costs of acting only on retaliation for prior attacks for defense.

This shift is not a cure; it is a curse. In pleading for preservation of the restrictive norms that prohibit preemptive strikes, historian Paul Schraeder, writing in *The American Conservative*, warns that the universal values "are changeable, fragile, gained only by great effort and through bitter lessons of history, and are easily destroyed, set aside, or changed for the worse for the sake of monetary gain or individual interest. And the fate of these norms and standards depends above all on what great powers, especially hegemons and superpowers do with them and to them. . . . The American example and standard for preemptive war, if carried out, would invite imitation and emulation, and get it. . . . A more dangerous, illegitimate norm and example can hardly be imagined. As could easily be shown by history, it completely subverts previous standards for judging the legitimacy of resorts to war, justifying any number of wars hitherto considered unjust and aggressive. [And] one can easily imagine plausible scenarios in which India could justly attack Pakistan or vice versa, or Israel or any one of its neighbors, or China Taiwan, or South Korea North Korea, under this rule that suspicion of what a hostile regime might do justifies launching preventive wars to overthrow it."

The Bush Administration has been vocal about the urgent need it perceives to do something about the dangers that confront U.S. security, but silent about the consequences that are likely to follow from that doctrinal shift to preemptive warfare. Do we really want to remove the normative handcuffs on the use of force? Do we really want to return to the freewheeling unrestricted sovereign right of any and all rulers to define for themselves when they are threatened, so as to license anticipatory preemptive warfare? Europe experimented with that Machiavellian basis for international statecraft in the 17th century during the deadly Thirty Years' War, which reduced its population by a third. Autonomy makes for global anarchy. Is severing normative anchors on permissible warfare that demonstrably have reduced its incidence really an idea that serves American and global interests and ideals? This radical departure in radical times looks increasingly like a path to peril and a road to ruin.

4

The U.S. Invasion of Iraq Was Based on False Pretenses

Charles V. Peña

Charles V. Peña is director of defense policy studies at the Cato Institute.

The March 2003 U.S.-led invasion of Iraq was based on the premise that Saddam Hussein's regime presented an imminent danger to democratic countries. To support this claim, in the weeks and months before the invasion, President George W. Bush assured America and the world that Iraq had large amounts of chemical and biological weapons and was intent on using them. As of July 2003, no weapons of mass destruction (WMD) have been found in Iraq, and much of what the Bush administration claimed about Iraq's WMD programs seems to have been false. But even if evidence of an Iraqi WMD program is found, the failure of Saddam Hussein's forces to use WMD during the invasion proves that his regime was not as great a threat as Bush had claimed.

[A s of July 2003,] weapons of mass destruction (WMD) have yet to be found in Iraq. At a minimum, this is an embarrassment for the Bush administration. And if WMD are eventually found, it won't matter because Iraq was not a threat to the United States in the first place—a point many observers gloss over.

WMD was the primary justification for launching a pre-emptive war against Iraq. Before the war, President Bush accused Iraq of having WMD and enough material "to produce over 25,000 liters of anthrax—enough doses to kill several million people . . . more than 38,000 liters of botulinum toxin—enough to subject millions of people to death by respiratory failure . . . as much as 500 tons of sarin, mustard and VX nerve agent." Secretary of State Colin Powell reinforced Bush's claims at a February [2003] presentation to the United Nations Security Council, where Powell provided photographic and audio intelligence as evidence to make the administration's case.

The current situation is rich with irony and contradiction. According to the administration, the U.N. weapons inspectors were incapable of finding any WMD because the Iraqi regime was engaged in an elaborate game of cat and mouse, moving weapons around to stay one step ahead of the inspectors (assuming they knew where to look in the first place). Furthermore, the inspectors were unable to interview scientists and officials with knowledge about WMD without fear of intimidation and retribution by Iraqi "minders."

If the Iraqis had chemical or biological weapons but did not use them to defend . . . against a foreign invader, how and when were they ever going to use such weapons?

Now, U.S. weapons inspectors have unimpeded access to Iraq. Most of the people who are supposed to know something about Iraq's WMD have been rounded up and are able to freely divulge their secrets. Yet the United States has been no more successful than the U.N.

The ultimate irony is Deputy Defense Secretary Paul Wolfowitz's statement that finding WMD in Iraq is "going to take time, and we're going to have to be patient." Time and patience are what the administration was unwilling to give the U.N. weapons inspectors.

The administration is confident that weapons will eventually be found. But what really matters, it says, is that the world is now a better place because the coalition has rid Iraq of an evil dictator and liberated the Iraqi people from his brutality. This revisionist rationale appears to satisfy most Americans. British Prime Minister Tony Blair—who is under fire from the Tory and Liberal Democrats and his own Labour Party, especially for his claim that Iraq had WMD that could be launched within 45 minutes—is repeating the same mantra, but not getting the same reception.

Senate and House intelligence committees have started closed-door hearings about the quality of the intelligence and how it was used by the Bush administration. A similar investigation is underway in the British Parliament. The obvious story in the making is about false premises for war and the potential fall from grace of Bush and Blair if WMD are not found in Iraq.

Any justification for the invasion?

The less obvious, but more important, story is if WMD are found in Iraq. The discovery of such weapons would not justify the war. Nor would it vindicate the administration because the administration will still have to explain how Iraq posed a direct and imminent threat to the United States. Defeating Iraq's military in three weeks is evidence that Iraq did not pose a military threat.

The possibility, acknowledged by Defense Secretary Donald Rumsfeld, that the Iraqis might have destroyed their WMD prior to or during the war only reinforces the notion that they were not a threat. More importantly, if the Iraqis had chemical or biological weapons but did not use them to defend their own country against a foreign invader, how and when were they ever going to use such weapons? Indeed, Saddam appears to have been deterred from using WMD to defend himself even as his regime was crumbling around him.

On a related note, it's clear that Iraq was not a hotbed of al Qaeda operations as was Afghanistan under the Taliban regime. Thus, the U.S. preoccupation with Iraq and WMD diverted America's attention from the real threat and what should be the focus of the war on terrorism: the al Qaeda terrorist network operating in 60 countries around the world.

Rand Beers, who recently quit as special assistant to the president for combating terrorism because he was disenchanted with the way the administration was handling the war on terrorism, believes the focus on Iraq has diverted manpower, brainpower, and money; created fissures in the alliance to fight the war on terrorism; and could breed a new generation of al Qaeda recruits. That is too high a price to pay in exchange for a wild goose chase for Iraqi WMD, which are much ado about nothing. They are weapons of mass distraction.

5

The U.S. Invasion
of Iraq Was Justified

Mansoor Ijaz

Mansoor Ijaz is a financier, op-ed columnist, and television commentator. He has written opinion pieces for the Los Angeles Times, *the* National Review, *and the* Washington Post.

Critics of the Bush administration have tried to make a scandal out of the U.S. failure to find weapons of mass destruction in post-invasion Iraq. However, the broader reason for forcing regime change in Iraq was that Iraqi leader Saddam Hussein was closely tied to global terrorism. Iraqi intelligence documents found in the aftermath of the invasion confirmed the scope of Saddam's efforts to contact and aid Osama bin Laden, head of the terrorist organization al-Qaeda. Furthermore, several known terrorists have been captured or found dead in post-invasion Iraq. Whether or not weapons of mass destruction are found in Iraq, it is clear that destroying Saddam Hussein's regime made the world a safer place.

From 1993 to 1998, the Clinton administration politicized intelligence on global terrorism and the rising power of al-Qaeda to such an extent that serious opportunities to dismantle Osama bin Laden's enterprise, and even capture him, were either ignored or purposely botched. I know, because I negotiated more than one opportunity—including with Sudan—and witnessed firsthand the games the Clinton White House played with the threats to our national security.

So it is fair game, today, to ask whether the Bush administration did the same—specifically, by playing fast and loose with evidence of Iraq's weapons of mass destruction [WMD]. Did we go to war with inadequate justification? President Bush's political opponents are making the most of the failure—so far—to find the WMD. But they are missing the larger picture, which is that Saddam Hussein was tied intimately to global terrorism. Blocked by sanctions, monitored by weapons inspectors (whom he kicked out when they got uncomfortably close to his secrets), and considered a pariah in most of the civilized world, Saddam needed bin Laden's network of suicidal individuals to distribute his recipes and formulas for (and even experimental doses of) weapons of mass terror to use against the U.S. and its allies.

Saddam's game plan almost worked, because most "experts" on terrorism convinced themselves there was an inadequate ideological basis for such an alliance with bin Laden—and it therefore couldn't exist. But in fact there was no important ideological difference between these terror czars; a common hatred for Israel and the U.S. was enough to seal their cooperation. Bin Laden viewed Saddam as an atheist without morals or scruples, and therefore not a threat to his global jihadist vision; Saddam viewed bin Laden as a useful lunatic whose acolytes could create havoc in the West with some plausibly deniable help from his scientists. All this could be achieved without any threat to Saddam's role as the chief pan-Arab nationalist leader.

Bin Laden's unholy alliance with Saddam was the most important reason to destroy Saddam's regime.

Finding Iraq's weapons of mass destruction may be a political imperative in Washington. But bin Laden's unholy alliance with Saddam was the most important reason to destroy Saddam's regime. And evidence uncovered after the Iraq war proves this alliance, and its potential purposes, beyond any reasonable doubt. Consider the following.

One. The Iraqis were intimately involved in helping al-Qaeda develop chemical-weapons capabilities—and this continues to have consequences. In early June [2003], ten letters laced with toxic powders were found in Belgium addressed to—among other targets—Prime Minister Guy Verhofstadt and the American, Saudi, and British embassies. All ten were sent by a little-known Islamic extremist group. Lab analyses of sickened postal workers who came into contact with the powder indicate that hydrazine and phenarsazine were present. Phenarsazine chloride is a precursor agent often used in mixing mustard gas or other nerve agents. This comes on the heels of the systematic dismantling of al-Qaeda's Ricin network by U.S. and European intelligence agencies in the months leading up to the Iraq war. That network had been fed recipes, expertise, and money by Abu Musab al-Zarqawi, a senior al-Qaeda biochemical-weapons expert who received urgent medical treatment in Baghdad last summer and then went into hiding in the Ansar al-Islam terrorist camps in northern Iraq. These camps, in which traces of Ricin were found on the soles of a shoe and boot recovered from the bombed-out wreckage, were populated by over 150 bin Laden-trained disciples. Zarqawi is now believed to be hiding out in Iran, where he may still be able to run parts of the European network that were not dismantled earlier this year.

Two. Documents found in the rubble of Iraq's Mukhabarat intelligence headquarters by reporters for London's *Daily Telegraph* show that Iraqi military and intelligence officials sought out al-Qaeda leaders much earlier than previously thought, and met with bin Laden on at least two occasions. In addition to previously reported meetings between Farouk Hijazi, a senior Iraqi intelligence officer, and bin Laden in Sudan in 1994, the

Mukhabarat documents show that on February 19, 1998, about six months prior to the attacks in Dar es Salaam and Nairobi, Iraqi intelligence officials made plans to bring a senior bin Laden aide to Baghdad from Khartoum. The key document shows that a recommendation was made for "the deputy director general [of Iraqi intelligence to] bring the [bin Laden] envoy to Iraq because we may find in this envoy a way to maintain contacts with bin Laden." The meetings took place in March 1998.

Concurrent with Saddam's outreach program to al-Qaeda was Sudan's almost desperate efforts to convince the Clinton administration to examine the intelligence they had gathered on everyone from bin Laden and his key deputy, Egyptian Islamic Jihad chief Ayman al-Zawahiri, to members of the Hamburg cell who provided aid to many of the 9/11 hijackers. Correspondence of February 1998 from Sudan's intelligence chief to the FBI's regional director went without reply until June 24, 1998, at which time the FBI sheepishly made it clear that the problem in communicating with Sudan lay elsewhere in the U.S. bureaucracy. The U.S. embassies were bombed six weeks later.

Three. Some of the world's most notorious terrorist villains have turned up in the postwar cleanup of Iraq. The legendary terrorist Abu Nidal committed "suicide" in Iraq last fall [2001]—supposedly by shooting himself in the head three times. His deputy, Abdul Rahman Isa, disappeared in an apparent kidnap in early September. In both cases, there was the strong smell of an effort to get rid of evidence—in the form of living terrorists on Iraqi soil—that could implicate Saddam.

But after the war, more of them emerged. Abu Abbas, mastermind of the 1985 Achille Lauro hijacking, was captured by U.S. forces. It turned out, further, that Abu-Zubayr, a senior al-Qaeda operative who had planned attacks on U.S. ships passing through the Straits of Gibraltar, was an officer in Iraq's secret police. In April [2003], U.S. forces in Baghdad also arrested Khala Khadr al-Salahat, the terrorist who allegedly had constructed the radio-sized bomb that blew up Pan Am Flight 103. In the rubble of the intelligence headquarters, evidence was found that the Iraqis had used their Manila embassy to funnel payments to al-Qaeda's Philippine operation, Abu Sayyaf; at Iraq's Salman Pak terror-training facility, an airplane was found that had been used to train hijackers.

One thing is clear from the postwar trove of intelligence on Saddam's ties to terrorists: When the world made it difficult for Saddam to hit his intended targets directly, he sought out others suitably inclined to do his dirty work. In some cases, he hid it well; in others he did not. But even the most diehard opponent of the war can no longer deny the physical evidence of the ties that bound Saddam to al-Qaeda and other terrorists, the scientific linkages that made them lethal, and the rationale for having to put an end to it all. The world is a much safer place thanks to the U.S. war to end this terror-sponsoring regime.

The United States Should Support Regime Change in Iran and Syria

Michael Ledeen

Michael Ledeen is a scholar at the American Enterprise Institute and the author of The War Against the Terror Masters.

President George W. Bush stated in the days after September 11, 2001, that the war on terrorism would be a long one, waged against all terrorist groups and their supporters. After the war on Iraq, the United States must turn its attention to Iran and Syria, the two major state sponsors of terrorism in the Middle East. Fortunately, the United States can encourage regime change in these countries without a military invasion. The United States should work to bring international political pressure against Syrian dictator Bashar Assad's oppression of the Syrian people and the citizens of Lebanon. In Iran, the United States should give political and economic support to the growing resistance movement, which in time will hopefully remove that country's tyrannical Islamic theocracy from power.

Editor's note: The following viewpoint was published on April 12, 2003, slightly less than a month after the start of the joint U.S.-U.K. invasion of Iraq. Ledeen's article originally appeared in the Spectator, *a British political magazine.*

The battle for Iraq is drawing to a close, but the war against terrorism has only just begun. As President George W. Bush has said since the first days after 11 September, this will be a long war, involving many terrorist organisations and many countries that support the terrorists. Saddam Hussein's Iraq was never the most threatening of those countries, even though Baghdad gave support to most of the world's leading terrorist organisations, and despite Saddam's programmes to develop weapons of mass destruction. That dubious honour belongs to Iran, three times the

Michael Ledeen, "The End of the Beginning," *The Spectator*, vol. 291, April 12, 2003, p. 14.

size of Iraq, flush with oil revenues, and the creator of modern Islamic terrorism in the form of Hezbollah, arguably the world's most lethal terrorist organisation. And then there is Syria, which has worked hand-in-glove with Iran to support Hezbollah—both in its terrorist garb (Hezbollah trains in the Bekaa Valley in Syrian-occupied Lebanon) and its political and philanthropic costume, in which Hezbollah members sit in the Lebanese parliament.

Today, both Iran and Syria are engaged in a desperate terrorist campaign against coalition forces in Iraq. The only surprise here is that so many diplomats and deep thinkers are surprised, for neither country has been reluctant to announce its intentions. Just over a week ago, for example, the Syrian dictator Bashar Assad incautiously told an interviewer that just because Iraq was conquered did not mean that the coalition had won. He said that the enemies of Britain and the United States would have to be patient, just as they were in Lebanon in the 1980s and 1990s, driving the United States and Israel out of the country by means of terrorist attacks. And Iran's supreme leader, Ali Khamenei, announced publicly that the presence of US forces in Iraq would be even worse than Saddam Hussein, arguably the man most hated by Iranians.

The strategy of a 'second Lebanon' was worked out over many months, during which there was a remarkable level of air travel between Baghdad, Damascus and Iran, involving leading diplomats, intelligence and military officers, and terrorist leaders. In the run-up to the invasion of Iraq, both Syria and Iran facilitated the movement of terrorists into Iraq: Syria was so bold as to give them Syrian passports, as coalition special forces discovered when they arrested the terrorists, while Iran typically covered its tracks by simultaneously enabling their passage to northern Iraq and then announcing it would arrest any terrorist it found.

It would be nice to believe that a combination of diplomatic and economic pressure will convince Syria and Iran to abandon their support of terrorism, but it's just not going to happen.

The joint strategy seems counter-intuitive to those who believe it is next to impossible for Sunnis and Shiites [two different sects of Islam] to co-operate, and that Iran could never co-operate with the regime of Saddam Hussein. But both Syria and Iran have good reason to contest the coalition victory. Assad and Khamenei have both heard Bush's reference to the 'Axis of Evil', and they have studied the many White House statements over the past year and a half. They have concluded that once the coalition victory is consolidated, they are next on the list. They believe they will have to fight for survival sooner or later, both against America's military and economic power, and against their own people, who they fear would be inspired by the spectacle of a free and independent Iraq to attempt a similar enterprise in their own countries.

They do not think they have any good soft option. The Americans are coming, and the Syrians and the Iranians are going to fight now, in Iraq. To be sure, they are not going to send their armies against us (quite aside from certain defeat, they no doubt fear massive defections), but rather a swarm of terrorists, from Hezbollah to Islamic Jihad, Hamas, al-Qa'eda, Ansar al-Islam, and the rest of the jihadist mafia. They have convinced themselves that this is a potentially winning strategy, both because of the Lebanon precedent and because of what they view as the increasing success of a similar campaign in Afghanistan.

Along with preparations for a terror war against the coalition, both Syria and Iran have ratcheted up the repression of their own domestic critics, even at the cost of antagonising foreigners, such as recent European Union human-rights and trade delegations in Tehran, who would prefer to ignore human-rights violations. Survival comes first, even for dictators who have demonstrated an enormous appetite for personal enrichment, and the Syrian and Iranian dictators are very worried.

Left undisturbed [the current regimes in Iran and Syria] will kill us in Iraq and Afghanistan, and will mount new attacks on our homelands.

Warnings have flowed from Washington in recent days, with the usual vigour and bluntness of the secretary of defense, Donald Rumsfeld, and the more modulated but nonetheless clear tones of the secretary of state, Colin Powell. These warnings signal something quite new in the war against terrorism, because heretofore the state department and the CIA had argued in favour of a sort of strategic engagement of both Damascus and Tehran. Top diplomats and intelligence analysts had maintained that the United States and Syria had common interests in fighting terrorism, since Osama bin Laden had condemned the Assad family's secular tyranny. And, despite the President's many harsh condemnations of Iran (an unelected regime defying the Iranian people's clearly expressed desire to be free), the state department continued to work for better relations with the mullahs. A few weeks ago this skeletal impulse was given flesh by the deputy secretary of state, Richard Armitage, who astonishingly proclaimed Iran 'a democracy' in a press interview.

So when both Powell and Rumsfeld come out swinging against the mullahs and the Assads, it is safe to assume that they have solid and abundant information to show that the 'second Lebanon' strategy is being implemented. The press has been given snippets of this data, from allegations that Saddam transferred weapons of mass destruction—and members of his family—to Syria before the outbreak of the war, to stories of thousands of Arab 'volunteers for Saddam' pouring across the border in quest of glorious martyrdom, to open questions about Iran's co-operation with Ansar al-Islam and al-Qa'eda.

So we can forget about the happy dream of being able to destroy the Baathist regime in Iraq, democratise the country, and then turn our attention elsewhere. We're in a regional struggle, and we are compelled to deal with it. It does no good to mutter that we should have seen it coming, and should have taken precautionary measures before the Iraqi campaign (we certainly had enough time). Here we are. Now what?

The short answer is: regime change. It would be nice to believe that a combination of diplomatic and economic pressure will convince Syria and Iran to abandon their support of terrorism, but it's just not going to happen. The Assads actually convinced Western governments that Syria did not actively support terrorist operations, but since 11 September a torrent of evidence to the contrary has been collected. My favourite comes from Germany, where court documents dealing with Jordanian terrorists based in Germany recount a trip of theirs to Syria, where they were arrested and interrogated by the defence minister, Mustafa Talas. At first he suspected them of being in cahoots with the Syrian Muslim Brotherhood—a sworn enemy of the regime—but when he found out that their leader was in Tehran, he gave them the phone number of Hamas, encouraged them to get in touch, and promised he had arranged the introduction.

Support for terror is an integral part of both regimes, and it is impossible to win the war on terrorism so long as the two regimes are in power. The good news is that both are very vulnerable to political attack.

In one of those delicious paradoxes that keeps historians in business, the soft underbelly of the Syrian regime is the very place Bashar Assad hailed as the model for the terrorist campaign against the coalition, namely Lebanon. The world knows that Lebanon is a military colony of Damascus, and, despite its parliamentary fig-leaf, is governed by the Syrian intelligence service. The Lebanese people have an historically legitimate claim to self-determination, and the West has abundant reason to endorse it. Some years ago, when the Syrian vice was closing on Lebanon, a Lebanese Christian leader held a press conference in which he delivered an unforgettable line: 'The Western world should either support us, or change its name.' The West did neither, falling into sin. Now there is an opportunity for redemption.

We should unleash the full panoply of political weapons on behalf of Lebanese freedom: a vigorous human-rights campaign, attention to the many stories of brutality and abuse coming from the lively Lebanese diaspora, political observers at every Lebanese election, demands for shutting down the infamous terrorist-training camps in the Bekaa Valley (where every terror group worthy of note has extensive facilities), investigations into the state of religious freedom, and so forth. Lebanese exiles should get special status, pending the liberation of their country.

Meanwhile, big brother should get similar treatment. Assad should be forced to account for the occupation of Lebanon. Perhaps one of those sanctimonious judges in Belgium or The Hague might have a look at the domination of Syria by an unelected regime from a minuscule sect. The Syrian people believe the Assads have billions of dollars stashed away in foreign bank accounts. If this is known, it should be publicised. If we have solid information that Iraqi weapons of mass destruction were moved into Syria, we should insist on proper investigation (this time with real investigators, not [chief weapons inspector for the United Nations Hans] Blix's keystone cops), or even organise one of those lightning operations at which special forces excel.

I do not believe that the Syrian people welcome dictatorship any more than the Iranians do, and the Iranians have made clear their hatred and contempt for the vicious mullahcracy that has wrecked their country over the last 23 years, all the while filling the pockets of the clerics. In Iran, we have a seemingly irresistible political card to play: give the people the same sort of political support we gave the Yugoslavs under [Slobodan] Milosevic, the Poles, Hungarians and Czechs under the Soviet empire, and the Filipinos under [Ferdinand] Marcos. We, and the Iranian people, want a peaceful transition from dictatorship to democracy, and it seems likely to succeed. There is even a suitable leader for the transition period: the late shah's son, Reza Pahlavi, who is widely admired inside Iran, despite his refreshing lack of avidity for power or wealth.

As President Bush has said, this war has a variety of targets and re-quires a variety of strategies. No one I know wants to wage war on Iran and Syria, but there is now a clear recognition that we must defend our-selves against them. They are an integral part of the terror network that produced 11 September. Left undisturbed they will kill us in Iraq and Af-ghanistan, and will mount new attacks on our homelands. We cannot give them time to organise these attacks, all the while developing the weapons we all properly dread. But unlike Iraq, there is no need for a mil-itary campaign. Our most potent weapons are the peoples of Syria and Iran, and they are primed, loaded and ready to fire. We should now pull the political lanyards and unleash democratic revolution on the terror masters in Damascus and Tehran.

7

The United States Should Not Support Regime Change in Iran and Syria

Part I: John Hughes; Part II: Flynt Leverett

John Hughes is a Pulitzer Prize–winning former editor of the Christian Science Monitor *and editor and chief operating officer of the* Deseret News. *Flynt Leverett is a former director for Middle East affairs at the National Security Council.*

Some foreign policy pundits have asked whether, after Iraq, Iran and Syria should be the next targets in America's war against terrorism. However, military intervention—or even open calls for regime change—would not be the best U.S. policy in either country. In Iran, vigorous diplomacy should be used to make it clear that Iran must not support terror, build weapons of mass destruction, and subvert the effort to rebuild Iraq. In Syria, U.S. diplomatic efforts can build upon Secretary of State Colin Powell's visit to Syria in May 2003. The United States should make it clear that it has no plans to attack Syria, but that it expects Syrian leaders to break their ties to terrorist groups like Hamas and Islamic Jihad. In the short term, the proximity of U.S. forces in Iraq should help keep both Iran and Syria in line, and in the long term, the establishment of a more democratic government in Iraq may help influence the entire Middle East.

I

George Bush is learning that he must use different tactics of varying subtlety as he positions the American megapower to deal with problems around the world.

In Afghanistan, it was regime removal. Knock out the Taliban and Al Qaeda and let freedom flourish.

In Iraq, it was regime destruction. Destroy the Saddam Hussein regime and replace it, at least initially, with American control.

In the Palestinian-Israeli imbroglio, it is regime change in the case of the Palestinians—freezing out Yasser Arafat and replacing him with Mahmoud Abbas. It is regime nudging in the case of Israel—nudging Prime Minister Ariel Sharon to a more cooperative position than he has ever been known to embrace.

In North Korea, where the compass has been swinging between diplomacy and war, it's now looking like a US demand for regime reform from within. Deputy Defense Secretary Paul Wolfowitz is floating the concept of China's example: How a failed communist state can reform without collapsing.

In the case of European allies, it is regime reward or regime retribution. Roses for Poland. For France, protestations of tough love but actually a raspberry. For Germany, a little time in the freezer. For Russia, well, Mr. Bush and President Vladimir Putin look like a couple of good ol' Texas boys making up after a wobbly Saturday night punch-up.

Which brings us to Iran, whose regime seems to have the Bush administration in a quandary. That quandary is exemplified by US indecision over the status of the People's Mujahideen, an Iranian resistance group operating from Iraq. It has been bombed and disarmed by the US, but it is now apparently finding favor from the US military although still listed by the State Department as a terrorist organization.

Iran is no friend of the US. Some hard-liners in the Bush administration are tempted to end its mischief by military means. The US did it in Iraq, why not in Iran?

But there are several reasons why this is not a good idea.

First, Bush faces a reelection campaign that, if it is to be successful, could do without the burden of occupying a new country of 65 million people with a long history of resentment against foreign invaders.

While there is much discontent in Iran with the influence of conservative clerics, its people have not been subjected to the brutal torture that terrorized Iraqis.

Second, the failure so far to find weapons of mass destruction and links to Al Qaeda in Iraq has produced credibility problems for the administration with the American public. It might undermine support for an assault on Iran justified on the same grounds. This does not mean that Americans have not cheered the demise of Saddam Hussein's wretched regime. It *does* mean that some of the reasons advanced to justify the regime's overthrow now seem less credible. Reasons for invading Iran would get sharper scrutiny.

Third, while the military campaign against Hussein was brilliant, the postwar economic and political reconstruction of Iraq so far is not. The US has much yet to do in Afghanistan, and a lot more to do in Iraq, before seeking a new venture of such magnitude in Iran.

Fourth, a US military adventure in Iran at this time would have an unsettling effect on the rest of the Islamic world and particularly on the

Palestinian-Israeli peace negotiations. Though not an Arab country, Iran is a Muslim country. Its occupation by the US would further impair the trust of Arabs that Bush seeks.

Fifth, while there is much discontent in Iran with the influence of conservative clerics, its people have not been subjected to the brutal torture that terrorized Iraqis. Some experts believe the Islamic revolution is tottering toward an end as a new generation of Iranians questions its legitimacy. This generation may yet do a better job of reforming its government than would the US Marines.

America's three reasonable requirements from Iran are that it not support terror, not build threatening weapons, and not subvert Iraq's teetering movement toward democracy.

Vigorous diplomacy should put these requirements front and center with the Iranian regime.

Vigorous public diplomacy should be brought to bear upon the 20-year-olds who are Iran's best hope for constructive change. A US-stimulated robust economy and movement toward democracy in neighboring Iraq would encourage them. A US-brokered peace deal between Palestinians and Israelis would help even more.

Iran's leaders can be under no illusions about the awesome military strength recently displayed by the US in Iraq. The close availability of that strength should be an incentive for Iran to respond to diplomacy so that the US doesn't have to use force.

II

The military victory over Saddam Hussein has empowered some officials in the Bush administration to push for similarly decisive action against other state sponsors of terrorism. For the hardliners, Syria has become the preferred next target in the war on terrorism. I know because I've been hearing the argument a lot in recent days.

For the last eight years, I have been directly involved in U.S. policy-making toward Syria, as a CIA analyst, on the State Department's policy planning staff and at the White House. In all that time, I have never seen officials as willing to take on the Syrian regime as they are today.

The current concern about Syria is understandable. A longtime supporter of terrorist groups, Syria has developed weapons of mass destruction. Moreover, Syria backed Saddam to the bitter end, challenging American interests.

But Syria also presents the administration with a strategic opportunity that would be imprudent not to explore. Since the Sept. 11 attacks, the problem of how to get states out of the terrorism business has been a defining question for American foreign policy.

In Afghanistan and Iraq, we Americans achieved this end by toppling irredeemable regimes. But can we change the behavior of a terrorism-sponsoring state like Syria without unseating its regime? Is it possible to reform Syria's posture not through force, but through diplomatic engagement?

The answer is a qualified yes. Secretary of State Colin Powell's visit to Damascus [on May 4, 2003] has the potential, I hope, to be the first stage in this experiment.

The success of engagement depends in large measure on Syria's president, Bashar Assad. Assad is not an ideological fanatic like Mullah Mohammad Omar, the Taliban leader, or an incorrigible thug like Saddam. He is young, educated partly in the West and married to a British-born woman who was once in J.P. Morgan's executive training program. He has also made it clear in private that Syria needs to modernize, and that its long-term interests would be served by better relations with the United States.

[Syrian leader Bashar Assad has] made it clear . . . that Syria needs to modernize, and that its long-term interests would be served by better relations with the United States.

While Assad's inclinations make engagement plausible as a strategy, constraints on his authority mean that diplomatic success is far from assured. Assad was only 34 when he became president upon the death of his father, Hafez, in June 2000. Until then, most of his political career had been spent as head of the Syrian Computer Society.

Still encumbered by several of his father's key advisers, he does not yet have the standing to make fundamental changes in policy on his own. One has only to observe the Syrian president in meetings where he is accompanied by his foreign minister (in office since 1984), his defense minister (in office since 1982) or his vice president (a key regime figure since the 1970s) to appreciate the constraints he faces.

For this reason, it will not be enough for U.S. officials simply to show up in Damascus, with a list of complaints about Syrian ties to Hezbollah and Hamas, and expect Assad to take action. Syria's leaders have heard these complaints before and have offered little more than canned rhetoric as a response.

This time Americans should avoid generalities and identify for Assad the specific steps he needs to take. These might include closing the Damascus offices of Palestinian terrorist groups like Hamas and Islamic Jihad, expelling terrorist leaders like Jihad's Ramadan Shallah, and stopping Iranian supplies for Hezbollah from moving through Syria on the way to Lebanon.

Americans should then outline a series of measures we would undertake if Syria fails to act. We might start with additional economic sanctions—such as barring Syria from participating in Iraqi reconstruction and imposing a comprehensive trade embargo—and end with covert and possibly overt attacks against terrorism-related targets in Syria or Lebanon.

But sticks alone will not produce more than short-term tactical adjustments in Syrian behavior. To bring about real change, we must also offer concrete benefits for meeting our demands. Doing so would enable Assad to demonstrate to the regime's inner circle that Syrian interests would be better served by cooperation with the United States rather than by confrontation. In this regard, an important incentive to offer Assad is a role in a strategic discussion about the region's future. After the 1991 Gulf War, Syria's principal forum for having its interests considered by the United States was the Syrian track of the Middle East peace process.

Since President Hafez Assad's death, there has been no Syrian track. Diplomatic marginalization has been a source of frustration for Syria—and it's one that will probably intensify as the country becomes encircled by pro-Western states—including, now, Iraq. We should therefore indicate a willingness to begin talking with Assad about Syria's regional interests, but only on the condition that he take steps to cut his country's links to terrorism.

We should also make clear that we would be prepared to remove Syria from the list of state sponsors of terrorism. In the 1990s, we made Syria's removal from the list contingent on a peace treaty with Israel that never came; we should now tie removal to changes in Syria's relations with terrorists. Taking Syria off the list would allow U.S. economic aid to flow to the country for the first time in decades and substantially increase assistance from international financial institutions.

Getting Syria out of the terrorism business through diplomacy would be a major achievement in itself, both for our counterterrorism campaign and our Middle East policy. Perhaps more significantly, success with Syria could establish hard-nosed engagement as the most effective way to confront, and eventually to change, the behavior of states that back terrorism.

8

The United States Must Crack Down on North Korea's Criminal Activities

Larry M. Wortzel

Larry M. Wortzel is vice president and director for the Heritage Foundation's Davis Institute for International Policy Studies and the author of The Chinese Armed Forces in the 21st Century.

The North Korean government headed by Kim Jong Il is actively engaged in drug trafficking, illegal missile sales around the world, and currency counterfeiting. It has also openly stated that it is pursuing the development of nuclear weapons. The nearly insolvent North Korean government is kept from collapsing largely by Communist China, which provides North Korea with much of its food and fuel. Therefore, effective economic sanctions against North Korea require Chinese cooperation. Military attacks against North Korea are an option for the United States, but direct U.S. action against North Korea could result in North Korean retaliation against South Korea or Japan, both U.S. allies. The United States must therefore insist on multilateral negotiations in its efforts to stop the dangerous activities of this rogue nation.

Editor's Note: The following viewpoint is excerpted from testimony that Wortzel gave before the Senate on May 20, 2003.

North Korea's exports from legitimate businesses in 2001 totaled just $650 million, according to *Wall Street Journal* reports of April 23, 2003, citing South Korea's central bank. Income to Pyongyang from illegal drugs in the same year ran between $500 million and $1 billion, while missile sales earned Pyongyang about $560 million in 2001. North Korea is producing some 40 tons of opium a year, according to U.S. Forces Korea officials cited in *The Guardian* on January 20, 2003, and earns some $100 million a year from counterfeiting currency.

Thus, like the regime of Saddam Hussein, the Kim Jong-il regime re-

Larry M. Wortzel, testimony before the Senate Governmental Affairs Subcommittee on Fiscal Management, Budget, and International Security, Washington, DC, May 20, 2003.

sembles a cult-based, family-run criminal enterprise rather than a government. And, like the former government of Saddam Hussein, the regime of Kim Jong-il operates with a complete disregard for international law and human life. The famine that Kim Jong-il permitted to continue in North Korea killed as many as 3 million people.

The disclosures now coming out about the way that Saddam Hussein and the Baath party ran Iraq show us what happens when a criminal gang takes over a nation and turns all of its resources to support the thugs in power. Unrestrained brutality, murder, torture, rape, and plunder were inflicted on the people of Iraq by the family of criminals from Tikrit. Of course, Saddam Hussein and his thugs could get rich and keep the state running because Iraq has so much oil. Kim Jong-il does the same to North Korea while kidnapping people from Japan and South Korea.

North Korea has no oil to export. In fact, it is one of the most repressed economies in the world, according to the *Index of Economic Freedom*, published annually by the *Wall Street Journal* and The Heritage Foundation. North Korea has no viable economy at all, its only major exports being dangerous weapons and dangerous drugs. To maintain himself in power, Kim Jong-il must ensure that the cadre of the Korean Workers Party, the North Korean People's Army, and the People's Security Force—his communist political base—are fed and have heat in the winter. Kim is aided in this goal primarily by the People's Republic of China [PRC], the communist leadership of which has vowed not to let North Korea collapse.

North Korea's international behavior and lack of a viable economy present a security dilemma of major consequence for the world. Our attention was most recently focused on the problem of North Korea's criminal behavior by the Australian Navy's apprehension of a North Korean ship carrying 110 pounds of heroin worth $50 million on April 20 [2003] in the Tasman Sea off Australia.

There are also persistent stories about North Korean diplomats carrying illegal drugs across borders in diplomatic pouches. In 1994, China stopped North Korean embassy employees smuggling 6 kilograms of North Korean–grown opium into China. In 1995, officials of the North Korean Ministry of People's Armed Forces were arrested by China. Austin Bay discusses these in a *Washington Times* opinion piece of May 15, 2003. The drugs are deadly, and the way that Pyongyang ships them around the world is but one of the indicators that under Kim Jong-il, North Korea is a rogue state. North Korea's behavior would be much more deadly if, instead of drugs and counterfeit money, Kim Jong-il was shipping weapons-grade nuclear material or nuclear weapons to terrorists and other failed states.

The drug trade

North Korea ships drugs everywhere. In my view, in a country where such strict government control is exercised over all aspects of personal and public life, such actions reflect a conscious government policy. The United States Department of State, in its annual *International Narcotics Control Strategy Report*, is reluctant to make that analytical judgment. In 1999, for instance, the State Department wrote that:

There have been regular reports from many official and unofficial sources for at least the last 20–30 years that the Democratic People's Republic of Korea encourages illicit opium cultivation and engages in trafficking of opiates and other narcotic drugs.

However, the State Department report goes on to say that "We have not been able to confirm the extent of North Korea's opium production, though we did receive one eye-witness report of 'large fields' of opium growing in North Korea." The State Department report in 1999 "estimated" that opium production in North Korea was between 30 metric tons and 44 metric tons.

Mr. Chairman [of the Senate], I find this statement shameful. Either American intelligence is inadequate, or the State Department can't bring itself to make a judgment call. If United States space surveillance assets cannot find and confirm the existence of opium poppies, which are brightly colored, seasonal, and grow above ground, we will never get adequate intelligence on North Korea's underground missile and nuclear weapons programs.

The Kim Jong-il regime resembles a cult-based, family-run criminal enterprise rather than a government.

North Korean diplomats, workers, and officials have been caught selling opiates—including heroin, amphetamines, and ryhopnol (known as the "date rape drug")—in Japan, China, Russia, Taiwan, Egypt, the Czech Republic, Bulgaria, and South Korea. Yet in its 2003 *International Narcotics Control Strategy Report*, the Department of State manages to conclude that there is "not conclusive evidence of illicit opium production in North Korea."

Mr. Chairman, as you may know, from 1988 to 1990, and then again from 1995 to 1997, I was a military attaché at the United States Embassy in China. During that period, I received a number of very credible reports from reliable sources of Chinese nuclear assistance to Pakistan and of the shipment of Chinese missiles and missile technology to Pakistan. Yet the Department of State could not conclusively say that there was such assistance until Pakistan tested its first missile and its nuclear weapons. I am a little skeptical of statements by the Department of State that "evidence is inconclusive."

In January 2002, Japanese officials seized 150 kilograms of methamphetamine from a North Korean vessel, and in July 2002, Taiwan government officials apprehended 9 men carrying 79 kilograms of heroin.

Clearly, Mr. Chairman, one way to put some pressure on North Korea is to mount a major international, worldwide diplomatic effort encouraging other countries to pay extra attention to North Korean drug trafficking and to apprehend those North Koreans, including diplomats, military, and government officials who transport and sell drugs. Even China, where the most senior officials of the People's Liberation Army have said that "China will not permit North Korea to collapse," is likely to assist in a concerted drug interdiction effort.

Shoring up a failed economy with counterfeit currency

North Korea's gross domestic product (GDP) in 2001 was US$15.7 billion. It exported $826 million in goods and imported $1,847 billion, leaving it a negative trade balance of –$1,021 billion.

North Korea has some brown coal but lacks coking coal and has no viable oil and gas deposits. The electric power transmission grid in North Korea loses about 30 percent of the power it transmits. One would think that any available funds would be used to upgrade this electrical transmission capacity. Instead, North Korea invested US$10 million in an intaglio printing press, the same type used by the United States Bureau of Engraving and Printing.

In 1999, the U.S. Congressional Research Service estimated that Pyongyang was producing and passing in foreign countries US$15 million a year in counterfeit currency. Pyongyang passes its fake bills everywhere. In April 1998, Russian police arrested a North Korean who was passing US$30,000 in counterfeit bills.

Missile sales

North Korea has exported significant ballistic missile–related equipment, parts, materials, and technical expertise to South America, Africa, the Middle East, South Asia, and North Africa. China has been a close partner of North Korea in missile sales, often teaming with the North when Pyongyang had specific "niche" capabilities sought by other countries.

Pyongyang has made some US$580 million in missile sales to the Middle East, but there are other regular customers for North Korean missiles. In 1993, Iran sought to acquire 150 Nodong-1 missiles (a variant of the Russian Scud) and also paid North Korea US$500 million for further missile development as well as technology for nuclear weapons. In August 1994, according to the publication *Iran Brief*, U.S. reconnaissance satellites captured images of three of these Nodong missiles being assembled 25 miles north of Esfahan, Iran. Zaire also concluded a US$100 million deal for North Korean missiles in 1994.

In 1995, the Central Intelligence Agency confirmed the transfer of a number of Scud transporter-erector-launchers (TELS) to Iran. In one reported deal, Iran proposed to pay for missiles from North Korea with oil. By 1997, China and North Korea were sending a joint team of technicians to Iran to work on the North Korean missile program.

There was also a set of barter arrangements between North Korea and Syria for missiles. Syria reportedly shipped Soviet SS-21 short-range ballistic missiles to North Korea, which Pyongyang planned to reverse engineer and use to improve the accuracy of the Scud missile.

The United States government believes that Pakistan's Ghauri missile (1,500-kilometer range) was based on technology and help provided by North Korea. In the case of Pakistan, from the late 1980s, China supplied nuclear-related technology and M-11 missiles while North Korea helped by providing expertise in the manufacture of the Ghauri, another class of missile. The Ghauri is a liquid-fueled version of the Nodong missile. In 1998, India stopped and detained a North Korean ship at Kandia that contained 148 crates of blueprints, machinery, and parts for ballistic missile production on the way to Pakistan.

As the world saw in December 2002, when the Spanish Navy intercepted a North Korean ship carrying parts for a dozen Scud missiles on the way to Yemen, the missile export problem can be particularly vexing. Compliance with the multilateral Missile Technology Control Regime is voluntary, and the sale of these missiles does not violate international law. Some have suggested the general quarantine of North Korean airspace and territorial seas to inspect ships and aircraft departing North Korea. I will discuss this option later in this testimony. . . .

The viability of military action, economic sanctions, and quarantine

An outright U.S. attack on North Korean missile facilities, nuclear facilities, or conventional forces is within the military capability of the United States; and it is an option that must always be available to the President. However, given the close proximity of some 20 million of South Korea's 42 million people to the Demilitarized Zone [the "neutral" zone between North and South Korea] where North Korea may have some 12,000 artillery pieces, such an action would exact a high cost in innocent civilian lives. It is estimated that based on the tremendous military might poised across the misnamed Demilitarized Zone, a million might be killed in just the opening days of a new war on the Korean peninsula between North and South Korea. Moreover, given U.S force dispositions in Japan, any attack on North Korea might well stimulate a response by Pyongyang on Japanese soil. Therefore, in my view, the close nature of the United States alliances with South Korea and Japan, respectively, means that these two nations must be consulted about any American military action toward North Korea.

An outright U.S. attack on North Korean missile facilities, nuclear facilities, or conventional forces . . . is an option that must always be available to the President.

China supplies between 70 percent and 88 percent of North Korea's fuel needs and some 30 percent to 40 percent of North Korea's food needs. Although the PRC government is said to have cut off fuel shipments to North Korea through the cross-border pipeline as a means to pressure Pyongyang into multilateral discussions among the United States, China, and North Korea, Beijing did not do so for long. Supposedly, there was a three-day "shut down" of oil transmission for technical reasons.

As I said earlier in this testimony, Mr. Chairman, the communist party leadership of the People's Republic of China has made a decision that it will not let the regime of Kim Jong-il collapse, and stopping food and fuel shipments to North Korea might bring about that collapse. This position by Beijing has been a steadfast one for 53 years, when China came to the assistance of North Korea in the Korean War.

China is also not much help in restraining North Korea's missile and nuclear exports. I believe that, regardless of the diplomatic rhetoric from

Beijing, China continues to support the proliferation of missiles and nuclear weapons to its allies. The basic policy of the Chinese Communist Party Politburo Standing Committee and its Central Military Commission since the mid-1950s has been that China should strive to break up what it characterizes as the "super-power" monopoly on such weapons. These policies undermine the security of the United States, frustrate or render ineffective American national security policies with respect to nonproliferation, and increase China's influence with a number of the "rogue states" around the world. Gaining China's full cooperation in restraining North Korea's behavior is difficult.

I do not believe that the negotiating position of the United States is advanced by direct, high-level bilateral talks between the United States and North Korea.

An air and sea quarantine of North Korea, or the inspection of all shipping out of North Korea, would be a difficult task to sustain. Such a quarantine would be an act of war, requiring the consent of Japan and South Korea since those two nations, our allies, would be most immediately threatened by a North Korean response. Where would the United States force a North Korean aircraft to land? Ships can be stopped at sea, but aircraft cannot be stopped in flight.

Practically speaking, though, no effective quarantine or inspection regime would be possible without the full cooperation of China and Russia. North Korea could simply opt to move its missiles, components, or experts through either or both of those two countries if China and Russia agreed to facilitate North Korean exports. While the United States may be able to secure the cooperation of Russia and China in stopping North Korea's illegal drugs from moving across their borders, I believe that China would not be a reliable partner in ending North Korea's missile and arms proliferation.

Policy recommendations

The patient, firm, and principled position of the Bush Administration is about right in my view. The United States should not pay blackmail to drug runners, counterfeiters, and the exporters of nuclear material and missiles. Any progress with North Korea and any economic assistance or help with the problem of electrical power must be predicated on the verifiable end of North Korea's nuclear program.

It is now clear that Kim Jong-il has not kept the agreements he made with South Korean president Kim Dae-jung during their [June 2002] summit in Pyongyang. Apparently, that summit was secured with the secret payment of US$500 million to Kim Jong-il before he would meet with South Korea's president. We all must stop paying blackmail.

I do not believe that the negotiating position of the United States is advanced by direct, high-level bilateral talks between the United States and North Korea. Such an approach only marginalizes South Korea and

Japan, which are American allies and are directly involved in the outcome of the security dilemma on the Korean peninsula. Furthermore, the United States should maintain its dignity when it negotiates. The U.S. Secretary of State has no place putting wreathes at the statue of Kim Il-sung and should not be doing the Macarena or the "Wave" in some stadium in Pyongyang.

Instead, we should:

- Work with the intelligence, customs, and law enforcement agencies of other countries, particularly those neighboring North Korea, to crack down on drug shipments. This improves the national security of all the countries that face the threat of dangerous illegal drugs.
- United States diplomats should stress that North Korea's drug trade is not an independent operation by a few criminals, but a controlled action by the Kim Jong-il regime.
- The sponsoring governments, to ensure that neither drugs nor counterfeit money pass out of North Korea through those embassies, must carefully monitor foreign diplomats in Pyongyang. North Korean diplomats abroad also must be carefully monitored.
- Just as we have done in the war on terrorism, the United States should work with international agencies and foreign governments to crack down on financial institutions that support North Korea's criminal activities, especially drug trafficking.
- Japan has some US$240 million in legal trade with North Korea. Legal trade should be the only way that North Korea can earn money, but if Pyongyang persists in illegal activities and refuses to return the families of the Japanese abducted by Kim Jong-il, U.S. public diplomacy should work to convince the Japanese people to cut off this trade.
- The United States must maintain a strong military presence in the Asia-Pacific region and be prepared to win any fight the North Koreans start.
- Additional ballistic missile defenses should be deployed in the region immediately, and missile defense research and development should be a priority for the United States and Japan.
- Negotiations with North Korea must be multilateral. The United States is not alone in facing North Korea.
- Any economic assistance to North Korea must be predicated on the verifiable end to its nuclear programs.

Keep up the pressure

The senior leaders of the Chinese Communist Party continue to support the negotiating position of North Korea in dealings with the United States. Both Pyongyang and Beijing insist that the only way to resolve the diplomatic and security dilemma is direct negotiations between the United States and North Korea. Seoul vacillates, privately seeking direct U.S.–North Korean talks. The United States cannot accept a nuclear North Korea.

I believe that bilateral negotiations are a mistake. Any solution to the nuclear program in North Korea must be multilateral. The same is true for addressing North Korea's economic problems. North Korea must make its own decisions about its nuclear program. United States diplomacy should be aimed at increasing the economic and political pressure on Pyongyang while the U.S. and allies maintain a strong military posture. If Pyongyang verifiably ends its programs, economic aid will follow.

North Korea is a vexing security challenge, but Pyongyang does not have the financial resources of Iran or Iraq. Without China's fuel and food aid, North Korea might be more willing to change the terms for diplomacy. As dangerous as North Korea is, however, it is a nation that has been essentially deterred since 1953 by a strong alliance between the United States and South Korea, by the U.S.-Japan alliance, and by a powerful U.S. military capability. The United States should not waver on any of these.

9

The United States Should Negotiate with North Korea

John Feffer

John Feffer is the editor of Power Trip: U.S. Unilateralism and Global Strategy After September 11, *and author of* North Korea, South Korea: U.S. Policy at a Time of Crisis.

Both President George W. Bush and North Korean leader Kim Jong Il, through their obstinacy in pursuing hard-line foreign policies, are threatening to create a serious military crisis in East Asia. The United States has refused to engage in diplomatic talks with North Korea since Bush took office, instead putting severe economic pressure on the country and encouraging Japan to use military pressure in the hopes of toppling the Kim Jong Il regime. North Korea, in turn, has engaged in drug trafficking and missile sales to support its economy while also pursuing the development of nuclear weapons in the hopes of gaining a bargaining chip with the United States. There is a solution to this growing crisis, but it requires that the United States and North Korea abandon their confrontational stances and engage in serious negotiations.

The streets of the capital are broad and the buildings monumental. Inside the grand state offices, a power struggle rages among the political elite, and the side that seems to have the upper hand is insulated, single-minded, and shamelessly belligerent. This clique supports a military-first policy that doesn't shrink from the first use of nuclear weapons, a stance that strikes fear into allies and adversaries alike. Nor are these fears soothed by the actions or rhetoric of the leader, a former playboy who owes his position to an irregular political process and the legacy of a more statesmanlike father.

Choose your capital: Pyongyang or Washington?

In the fun house of mirrors in which contemporary global politics is enacted, a strange resemblance has developed between George W. Bush and Kim Jong Il and between their respective war parties. That North Korea is one of the poorest and most desperate countries in the world and the U.S. is the undisputed economic and military leader makes this *folie à deux* [shared delusion] all the more poignant and ridiculous. The weaker side has excited the Non-Proliferation Treaty [under which North Korea pledged not to acquire or develop nuclear weapons] and is rushing to develop a nuclear deterrent; the stronger side is after nothing less than regime change. This summer [2003] Washington is confronting Pyongyang with a policy of naval interdiction and a tightening chokehold of economic isolation. North Korea is perilously close to treating these encroachments on its sovereignty as tantamount to war. Neither side trusts the other; both refuse to blink.

Such a convergence of opposites is not unheard of in international relations. During the cold war, for instance, the U.S. and the Soviet Union both indulged in a terrifying symmetry of nuclear deterrence, third world interventions, and mistaken budget priorities. But even during the darkest days, Reagan and [Soviet leader] Gorbachev displayed a personal rapport. In contrast, George W. Bush has called Kim Jong Il a "pygmy" and a "spoiled child" and has confessed to journalist Bob Woodward that he wants to topple the regime in Pyongyang regardless of the consequences. North Korea has repeatedly warned of turning Washington (or Seoul or Tokyo) into a "sea of fire." The extraordinary gap in military and economic capabilities, like a difference in electric potential, has already produced sparks that may yet lead to a conflagration.

In East Asia, the cold war is not over, and the conflict between Pyongyang and Washington, with its dance of dependency and reciprocity, threatens to spiral out of control in ways that Afghanistan and Iraq (so far) have not. War on the Korean Peninsula would be catastrophic enough. But by encouraging Japan toward a military renaissance and pressuring South Korea to back a policy of isolating North Korea, the Bush administration is pushing all of East Asia to the brink.

Policy shift

In the fall of 2000, when the presidency of George W. Bush was just a glint in the eye of Florida's secretary of state, the U.S. and North Korea nearly ended their 50-year war. Madeleine Albright visited Pyongyang in October and found Kim Jong Il "very decisive and practical and serious." Bill Clinton was slated to meet the North Korean leader to conclude a grand deal that would have traded economic incentives and security assurances for an end to North Korea's missile programs. This deal would have built on the 1994 Agreed Framework, also negotiated by the Clinton administration, which froze the country's nuclear program in exchange for two light-water reactors, shipments of heavy fuel oil, and steps toward diplomatic normalization.

Clinton didn't go to Pyongyang, and the grand deal didn't materialize. Instead, the Bush administration took over with a determination to upend what it considered Clinton's policy of "appeasement." It was aided in this quest by a piece of intelligence inherited from its predecessor, namely that North Korea had taken out a nuclear insurance policy. Although its plutonium processing facility remained frozen, North Korea was exploring a second route to the bomb through uranium enrichment. The Bush team thus had the perfect weapon to attack U.S.–North Korean reconciliation: the perfidy of the North Koreans themselves.

But the U.S. had also backtracked on promises. It never fully lifted economic sanctions against North Korea and didn't take other steps toward the normalization of diplomatic relations suggested by the Agreed Framework. The Clinton administration persuaded Congress to accept the construction of two light-water reactors in North Korea by arguing, quietly, that the regime in Pyongyang would not likely be around in 2003 when the reactors were supposed to go online. Instead, the regime is still around, and the reactors are only one-third complete.

Although North Korea pursued its enriched uranium program in the latter days of the Clinton administration, analysts Joel Wit and James Laney suggest that the program accelerated only when the Bush administration cranked up its hostile rhetoric—suspending diplomatic contact, criticizing [former South Korean president] Kim Dae Jung's engagement policy, and ultimately including Pyongyang in its infamous "axis or evil." Whatever doubts remained in Pyonyang about U.S. intentions were dispelled by the war in Iraq, which led North Korean leaders to draw three conclusions. A nonaggression agreement with the U.S. was pointless. No inspections regime would ever be good enough for Washington. And only a nuclear weapon would deter a U.S. intervention.

North Korean threat?

This spring [2003] North Korea declared that it had acquired this ultimate deterrent. Beyond the declaration, however, the evidence is scant. Even if North Korea had enough fissionable uranium or plutonium, the material would need to be weaponized, which requires miniaturization technology that North Korean scientists do not likely possess. A CIA report recently leaked to *The New York Times* suggests that North Korea has an advanced nuclear testing site in Yongdok, but there is still no evidence that Pyongyang has yet developed any warheads to test. As for delivering such a weapon, North Korea has tested only one rocket with the potential to reach parts of Alaska—the Taepodong in 1998—and the launch fell far short in terms of both distance and accuracy. Nor does North Korea likely have the heat shield technology that would prevent its warheads from burning up on reentry from the atmosphere.

Pyongyang believes that it needs a nuclear weapon—or the much cheaper illusion of one—because its conventional forces are a mess. Though superior to the South Korean Army on the eve of the Korean War, North Korean forces have fallen on hard times. The South Korean Army spends $163,000 per soldier for food, clothes, and armaments. North Korea spends less than one-tenth that amount. North Korea's entire government budget is several billion dollars smaller than South Korea's military budget alone. Underfunded and no longer aided by cheap Soviet imports, North Korean military technology is out-of-date. In a naval battle in 1999, South Korean forces easily outgunned the North Koreans. A South Korean officer told the *Korea Herald*, "You could see many North Korean sailors exposed on the deck, because they had to handle the guns manually, while our sailors were inside watching radar screens and computer monitors." Without fuel or spare parts, North Korean pilots are limited to thirteen hours of training missions a year. After five years of food shortages, soldiers are malnourished, and many have been rebuilding crumbling civilian infrastructure rather than training in military exercises.

Even so, Pyongyang is not entirely a paper tiger. Its stocks of short-range missiles and long-range artillery could do a great deal of damage, particularly to South Korea. To beef up this retaliatory capability, Pyongyang continues to finance its military sector, thus diverting precious funds away from stabilizing its economy. The worst of the famine that plagued the country after 1995 is over, but the North Korean economy remains fragile. And the Bush administration wants to cripple North Korea's economy further still.

Economic noose

It's never been easy to get from Japan to North Korea. Most visitors have to fly to Beijing before boarding a biweekly North Korean jetliner to Pyongyang. By sea, however, several cargo ships and a weekly ferry have until recently carried people and goods between the two countries. Most of this trade has been overseen by Chosen Soren, an association of Koreans affiliated with Pyongyang but living in Japan.

In early June [2003], nearly 2,000 Japanese government inspectors descended on the docks of Niigata, a port on the western coast of Japan, in preparation to search the incoming North Korean ferry for safety violations, infectious diseases, and immigration irregularities. Pyongyang responded by canceling the ferry run. Urged on by Washington, the Japanese authorities also detained two North Korean cargo ships as part of an effort to shut down trade relations between Chosen Soren and Pyongyang.

The Bush administration is pushing all of East Asia to the brink.

As summer approached, Washington and Tokyo shifted into high gear to turn the economic screws on North Korea. The military option remains on the Pentagon's table, but Washington is also testing the possibility of toppling the regime in Pyongyang by spending it into the ground.

This economic strategy has several components. The Bush administration has cut back on food aid, arguing that monitoring should be improved and no doubt hoping that fewer high-calorie biscuits will incite children, pregnant and nursing mothers, and the elderly to rebel against the regime. There has also been an attempt to cut off the drug trafficking and arms exports that North Korea has increasingly relied on, in part because Pyongyang's attempt to expand legitimate enterprises has been thwarted by the U.S. and its allies. Toward that end, in June Washington developed the "Madrid initiative" by convening another coalition of the willing to explore how to bend international law to the U.S. objective of boarding every suspicious vessel heading into and out of North Korea.

And the otherwise-multilateralism-averse Bush administration is rejecting North Korea's demand for bilateral negotiations in favor of including more countries in the discussion. This strategy serves to underscore North Korea's isolation. But the hard-liners in the administration—John

Bolton in the State Department, Paul Wolfowitz in the Pentagon—are also not interested in the give-and-take of negotiations. This "just say no" faction has repeatedly rebuffed various North Korean offers, not bothering to pursue the negotiable items beneath the bluff and bluster in an effort to achieve a diplomatic solution to the escalating crisis.

Military shell game

In the fall and winter of 2002, hundreds of thousands of South Koreans poured into the streets to protest the acquittal of two U.S. soldiers whose vehicle struck and killed a pair of young Korean girls. Many of the protestors also wanted a reduction of the 37,000 troops stationed in South Korea, nearly half of whom are positioned as a tripwire near the demilitarized zone (DMZ) across from North Korea.

Imagine Korea's surprise when the U.S. military responded this June [2003] by announcing the withdrawal of the Second Infantry Division from the DMZ to positions south of Seoul. The protestors should have been delighted. They weren't.

Although the transformation of U.S. forces in South Korea to a more mobile rapid reaction force has been underway for several years, the withdrawal of the troops from the DMZ has been widely interpreted as pulling U.S. soldiers out of harm's way to prepare for a military strike on North Korea. The Pentagon has long been concerned with the "tyranny of proximity" that hampers its maneuverability on the Korean Peninsula.

New South Korean President Roh Moo-Hyun pleaded with Washington to put off this relocation until the current nuclear crisis is resolved. He was ignored. Instead, the Bush administration threw money at the problem, offering $11 billion to upgrade U.S. forces in South Korea over the next four years.

This latest offer is part of a joint U.S. and South Korean effort to beef up the latter's military capabilities. Seoul has set out to acquire at least three Aegis-class destroyers and to upgrade its air force with cutting edge U.S. reconnaissance planes and F-15 fighters. At South Korea's urging, the U.S. reversed a 1979 agreement and extended the range of South Korean tactical missiles to 300 km, which brought them within striking distance of all of North Korea. For 2003, the Seoul government will spend $14.5 billion on the military, a 6.4% increase over 2002 and the highest defense budget in its history.

The North Korean threat serves as a useful rationale for missile defense and the expansion of U.S. military influence in East Asia.

South Korea is not the only country in the region to use the current crisis as a rationale for military muscle flexing. In February 2003, for the first time since World War II, a top Japanese official threatened another country with attack. Defense Minister Shigeru Ishiba argued that Japan had the right to prevent a North Korean ballistic missile attack. What Ishiba failed to explain was how Japan was going to accomplish this preemptive strike. Still governed by a peace Constitution that restricts its military to a defensive posture, Japan has no offensive missiles of its own. And without an in-air refueling capacity, Japanese bombers can only make one-way trips.

Until the U.S. and North Korea [get] serious at the negotiating table, East Asia will remain on the precipice.

All of that is changing. Under the leadership of Prime Minister Junichiro Koizumi and with support from Washington, Japan is shrugging off the constraints of its peace Constitution. It is aggressively pursuing missile defense, has launched its first military satellites, has promised to provide backup to any U.S. military action in the region, and is set to acquire an in-air refueling capacity to make its threats of preemptive strikes a great deal more credible. Some Japanese and U.S. politicians have even called on Tokyo to develop its own nuclear deterrent.

Disturbing parallels

By bolstering allied forces in South Korea and encouraging Japan to flex some newfound offensive muscles, the U.S. is following through on its own military-first policy. The parallel with Pyongyang is disturbing. Until recently, North Korea pursued a strategy of *kangsong taeguk*, seeking strong economic and military power. Building up the military was important, but so too were the critical economic reforms that the government had been slowly unveiling in preparation for the big bang of lifting wage and price controls in summer 2002. In March 2003, however, Pyongyang shifted to a military-first policy in response to the current crisis.

The hard-liners in both capitals have developed a reckless codependency. The North Korean threat serves as a useful rationale for missile defense and the expansion of U.S. military influence in East Asia. And obstinate leaders in Pyongyang, who blame U.S. policies for the problems that assail the country, now have ample ammunition for their argument that negotiations with Washington are a waste of time.

It is difficult to know what kind of opposition to this inflexible position exists in Pyongyang. In Washington, though, bipartisan support for a diplomatic solution is growing. Conservative Republican Rep. Curt Weldon visited Pyongyang in June and came back with a ten-point proposal that would start with a one-year nonaggression pact signed by Washington and Pyongyang. Within the administration, it is rumored that the relatively moderate Colin Powell and his allies in the State Department continue to push for the more traditional carrot-and-stick policies of the Clinton era. Scholars and activists are also mounting pressure from the outside.

A bipartisan consensus has formed around a revised "grand bargain" between the U.S. and North Korea that would freeze the latter's nuclear and missile programs in exchange for political and economic incentives. According to this new consensus, promoted for instance by Selig Harrison and the Task Force on U.S. Korea Policy, North Korea would freeze both its plutonium reprocessing and uranium enrichment facilities in exchange for guaranteed supplies of energy (such as natural gas from Russia), and it would freeze its missile testing program in exchange for U.S. or European launches of North Korean satellites. In addition, the U.S. would finally lift all remaining sanctions against North Korea, support North Korea's applications to international financial institutions, and provide economic support for the rehabilitation of North Korea's energy and extraction industries. The U.S. would also eventually "lower its military profile" on the peninsula in exchange for comparable confidence building moves by North Korea.

Considered in isolation, many of the elements of this grand bargain are certainly within reach. In October 2002, North Korea offered to shut down its nuclear program in exchange for a nonaggression pact, and it has indicated on numerous occasions that its missile program is negotiable. In 2000, North Korea made an opening bid to end its missile program in return for $3 billion over three years, no doubt a negotiable figure. It also wouldn't take much to remove North Korea from the State Department's terrorism list and to lift the remaining economic sanctions. North Korea has hinted that it would compromise on the single remaining obstacle—several Japanese Red Army hijackers holed up in North Korea for the last 30 years. [In 1970 the Japanese Red Army (JRA), a Japanese terrorist group, hijacked a Japan Airlines airliner and forced it to land Pyongyang. Most of the hijackers are still living in North Korea.]

Before the current crisis broke, such a grand bargain with North Korea seemed conceivable. Other countries—South Korea, Taiwan, South Africa, Kazakhstan—have been persuaded to stop nuclear programs through diplomatic means, and the right combination of incentives no doubt could have been found for North Korea. Now, however, an Agreed Framework Plus that could provide such a magical mix of carrots seems almost chimerical owing to the twin obsessions of the principals—Washington's push for regime change and Pyongyang's pursuit of nuclear deterrence. We are entering a crushing new era of geopolitics. In the absence of well-enforced international laws and treaties, countries will fall back on their own mechanisms for preventing outside intervention. In geopolitics, as in geometry, parallel tracks do not meet. Until the U.S. and North Korea undo their fearful symmetry by getting serious at the negotiating table, East Asia will remain on the precipice.

10

The United States Should Press for Peace in Sudan

Walter H. Kansteiner

Walter H. Kansteiner is the U.S. Department of State assistant secretary for African affairs.

Sudan has been embroiled in a bloody civil war since 1983, as the ruling government and the Sudan People's Liberation Army (SPLA) have vied for power. The war has resulted in famine, slave trading, and ethnic cleansing. The Sudanese government has been the main perpetrator of human rights abuses. It has also allowed itself to become an international base for terrorists, including at one time al-Qaeda leader Osama bin Laden. The goals of the United States in Sudan are to 1) deny terrorists the use of Sudan as a safe harbor, 2) ensure that humanitarian relief groups have access to the nation, particularly southern Sudan, and 3) support a settlement of the ongoing Sudanese civil war. Achieving peace and stability in Sudan will benefit both the United States and the Sudanese people. Therefore, the United States must make a long-term commitment to the Sudanese peace process.

I am honored to have the opportunity to appear before this Committee to discuss . . . one of the greatest humanitarian tragedies in the world. The oft-quoted statistics on Sudan—36 years of civil war in 46 years of independence, two million dead, four million internally displaced, 500,000 refugees—are numbing in their magnitude. Slave raiding, aerial bombing of civilians, attacks on relief centers, pillaging of aid supplies, use of food as a weapon of war, forced displacement of populations, interference with religious freedom, any of these would guarantee a country a prominent spot on the dismal map of human suffering, but in Sudan we see all these horrors together enacted and reenacted.

Those who have seen the misery of that country's people know that the United States of America cannot ignore what is going on there. Sudan must be a priority in America's foreign policy. I can assure this Committee that it is.

Walter H. Kansteiner, testimony before the House International Relations Committee, Washington, DC, June 5, 2002.

U.S. interests in Sudan

The Administration's Sudan policy is multifaceted in its approach to key U.S. strategic interests and its support for the ideals and compassion of the American people. We will seek to deny Sudan as a base of operations for international terrorism even as we work to bring about a just and lasting peace, push for unhindered humanitarian access, and improved human rights and religious freedom. These goals represent a complex balancing act which I will try to make a bit clearer through my remarks. What I hope is immediately clear is the need for your continued support as we aggressively pursue an end to the suffering which has tragically marked the lives of too many Sudanese people.

Protecting the American people from any and all threats that may emanate from Africa must be a primary policy focus. The events of September 11 [2001] and Africa's own sad experience with the [1998] terrorist attacks against our embassies in Kenya and Tanzania necessitate that counter-terrorism concerns remain front and center as an issue in our diplomatic relations with the Government of Sudan. The Department's recent release of the *Patterns of Global Terrorism* report points to our sustained vigilance. While the report does refer to a measurable increase in counter-terrorism cooperation with Sudan, we remain concerned by the government's ongoing tolerance of and support for groups such as Hamas and Palestinian Islamic Jihad. However, due to the sensitive nature of this subject and ongoing discussions, I recommend a different forum for detailed briefings on this matter.

We will seek to deny Sudan as a base of operations for international terrorism even as we work to bring about a just and lasting peace.

As important as our counter-terrorism efforts remain in Sudan, our quest for a just peace, sustained humanitarian access, and dramatic improvements in human rights are a direct reflection of the principles embraced by the American people and pursued through the leadership of President [George W.] Bush. In September 2001, President Bush named Senator John Danforth the Special Envoy for Peace in Sudan. In fulfilling his mandate, Senator Danforth has advised that the parties to the conflict have shown sufficient will to engage in a peace process. We must now work diligently to demand deeds rather than mere words, and in this regard the government in Khartoum [capital of Sudan] will have much to prove. President Bush has asked Senator Danforth to continue on as his envoy for peace in Sudan as we push for a just peace. The United States considers the onus of ending the civil war squarely on the shoulders of the government.

The road to peace will be arduous and long, and President Bush has clearly articulated an immediate need for relief for the millions of Sudanese who suffer needlessly. In support of that effort, the President appointed USAID [United States Agency for International Development] Administrator, Andrew Natsios, Special Humanitarian Coordinator and tasked him with developing and implementing strategies that would alleviate the dire humanitarian situation at hand. In this vein, I will add that USAID, particularly OFDA [Office of Foreign Disaster Assistance], under the leadership of Roger Winter, has played a critical and outstanding role in moving forward on Sudan. His value as a partner in our efforts cannot be overstated.

The humanitarian crisis

There is an inextricable link between our search for peace and more proximate gains in the areas of humanitarian access and respect for human rights. These gains will be incremental but represent an essential operationalization of our overall efforts. We seek sustained and measurable achievements in pursuing: 1. A cease-fire and humanitarian access to the Nuba Mountains area; 2. Zones and periods of tranquility for humanitarian access; 3. The introduction of an international commission to investigate slavery, abductions and forced servitude; and 4. The cessation of attacks on civilians. The commitments that the parties have made to implement these agreements will necessarily represent ongoing tests of their will to cooperate in good faith. While not perfect, these tests represent unprecedented progress which, most importantly, continues to save lives.

The United States remains the leading donor of humanitarian relief to Sudan and we will continue to take this lead—including to northern victims of drought—whenever and wherever possible. We are working to move through barriers to our relief efforts, whether imposed by Khartoum or other parties to the conflict. I note again the Administration's clear view that cooperation on humanitarian delivery cannot be delinked from our overall understanding of the parties' commitment to work with the United States and others to advance peace. . . . I would like to highlight an important accomplishment in our engagement so far. We have secured access to areas that have been previously "off limits," like the Nuba Mountains. This area has not seen significant humanitarian relief in more than eight years. The cease-fire, coupled with scaled-up humanitarian access, has breathed life into a devastated area and allowed the people of Nuba to reach some measure of equilibrium.

Maintaining our commitment to those that suffer at the hands of the government in Khartoum also means forthrightly denouncing the egregious human rights violations that occur in Sudan. The practice of slavery in the Sudan cannot be denounced strongly enough and the Sudanese government's tolerance for the practice is simply unacceptable. The recently completed findings by the U.S.-led International Commission to Investigate Slavery, Abductions and Forced Servitude demonstrate that there is no question that slavery continues to occur in Sudan today and that it is perpetrated by people who, when not acting in concert with government forces, at least enjoy government forbearance. No one has been arrested, much less prosecuted, for this crime. The message of the Sudanese government is not that this horror must end, but that Sudan's critics fail to appreciate the unique cultural circumstances that give rise to "abductions." We do not, nor will we ever, accept this argument. The findings of the Commission address this cynical and unacceptable response and deny the government semantic latitude when answering for

their actions in international fora. The report also lays out a series of recommendations that the Sudanese government must take to stop the attacks, free the victims, and punish the guilty.

This is merely one example of the pervasive violations of human
rights that typify Sudan. All the belligerents, to one degree or another,
have made civilians targets in this war, but no party bears a heavier responsibility than the Sudanese government. The most contentious of the
Danforth initiatives addressed this issue specifically. In February 2002,
the government and the SPLA agreed to cease attacks on civilians in ac-
cordance with the rules of war as outlined in the Geneva Convention. We
are in the process of installing an on-the-ground monitoring mechanism
to determine the belligerents' commitment to this agreement. Although
reported violations of this agreement by both sides have been cataloged,
we will persist in establishing the monitoring mechanism simply because
it allows the international community unprecedented access and a clearer
picture of the situation. We thank you for your cooperation and participation in making funding available to implement these mechanisms and
will keep Congress informed as this process evolves.

---

*The human rights and humanitarian crisis in Sudan
has its basis in the ongoing civil war.*

The human rights and humanitarian crisis in Sudan has its basis in
the ongoing civil war. The environment in which the humanitarian
crises, the religious persecution, and the disregard for human rights exist
results from government and opposition resolve to settle their differences
militarily. The duration and nature of the civil war, however, make it
clear that neither the government nor the opposition can win militarily.
Without a strong international role, it is doubtful the parties to the conflict possess the initiative necessary to resolve the differences of their own
accord. This is where we have focused our diplomatic efforts.

We appreciate that none of Sudan's problems exist in a vacuum. So
long as the civil war goes on, the suffering of the civilians will continue.
I cannot put it more directly or forcefully than has Deputy Secretary [of
State] Armitage: we have got to try to stop the war.

Leading the peace process

The release of Senator Danforth's report [in April 2002] marks the initial
step to determine if we can indeed stop the war. His initial mandate, as I
mentioned earlier, was to determine if the parties to the conflict are
earnest in their stated desire for peace. Senator Danforth found that while
the parties have demonstrated an ability to reach agreement on contentious issues, the difficulty of achieving these agreements underscores
the necessity of outside intermediaries. Specifically, and in short, he notes
that the time is right for the United States to participate and act as a cat-
alyst in a peace process. The Administration agrees with his conclusion.

In charting a course for a peace process, the United States is closely coordinating with Kenya, the United Kingdom, Norway, Switzerland, Egypt

and others. The consensus among the parties to the conflict and countries coordinating with the United States is that instead of introducing an entirely new proposal, peace negotiations will only develop momentum and succeed if they are undertaken through an existing framework to which both parties are agreed in principle. The nascent Intergovernmental Authority on Development (IGAD) framework is the only vehicle for peace that fits this need at this time. Having stalled in the past due to a lack of broad participation, both the parties to the conflict and the coordinating partners agree that the IGAD framework, with several key points of the Egyptian-Libyan Initiative (ELI) included, is the strongest and most viable forum for peace discussions. More importantly, the IGAD framework is the only agreement signed by both parties to the conflict that resolves and acknowledges critical issues like self-determination for the south, religion and state, and governance.

When we talk about the prospects for peace in Sudan, we must be realistic, and we must be prepared for a long-term commitment. The latest iteration of this war is 19 years old. Achieving a just peace will require resolution of difficult questions such as the role of religion in the state, boundaries, sharing of oil revenue, and guaranteeing respect for the south's legitimate right to self-determination. Peace negotiations will require sustained effort and the demonstration of a will to peace that appears so far to be less than enthusiastic. Although a comprehensive cease-fire would be an important milestone on the way to a just peace, it must be a viable, negotiated cease-fire that advances the search for a comprehensive settlement. The Sudanese government's frequent calls for a cease-fire appear to be tactical posturing rather than indications of a move toward a just peace. A serious cease-fire would, first and foremost, be integrated into a peace process. It would also address the military issues on the ground such as re-supply of troops, importation of arms, and monitoring of troop movements. A cease-fire that does not speak to those sorts of issues will be as short-lived as the various humanitarian cease-fires or bombing halts that have come and quickly gone over the years.

Humanitarian relief, human rights, and peace are three critical keys to our Sudan policy. We must work on all three simultaneously, but we must insist on concrete progress by all the parties. To achieve our goals, we must be prepared to aggressively advocate our positions in Khartoum. We have been looking at re-staffing our Embassy in Khartoum to provide the presence we need to advance our interests there and to support an engagement on the issue of peace. Our efforts to do so have been with our eyes wide open. The Sudanese conflict has gone on too long. Along with key allies—the United Kingdom, Norway, Kenya, Switzerland, and others—we are committed to pushing all of the key actors to a serious, comprehensive and hopefully lasting, peace process.

11

U.S. Peace Efforts in Sudan Are Biased

Sharif Hikmat Nashashibi

Sharif Hikmat Nashashibi is managing editor of the Middle East Times *and chairman of Arab Media Watch, an organization dedicated to objective British coverage of Arab issues.*

In October 2002 Congress passed the Sudan Peace Act, intended to bolster U.S. efforts to help end Sudan's civil war. Specifically, the act authorizes funding for humanitarian efforts in Sudan and empowers the United States to institute a variety of economic sanctions against Sudan if, in the view of the United States, both sides of the Sudanese civil war are not negotiating in good faith. However, the United States is biased against the Islamic government of Sudan, and in favor of the rebels in the conflict, the Sudan People's Liberation Army (SPLA). The humanitarian relief efforts that the United States supports mostly help the SPLA, while sanctions threatened by the Sudan Peace Act would mostly hurt the government and innocent Arabs. The Sudan Peace Act is simply a cover under which the United States will meddle in Sudan's internal affairs in order to further its own agenda.

U.S. President George W. Bush signed legislation on October 21 [2002] calling for sanctions on Sudan if he finds that negotiations to end the country's 19-year civil war are not being conducted in good faith. One would logically assume that this applies to both parties to the conflict, but unfortunately, Bush and logic have never been fond of each other. Washington's Sudan Peace Act stipulates that the onus lie solely with the government in Khartoum [the capital of Sudan].

Biannually, should Bush find that the government is acting in bad faith or has "unreasonably interfered with humanitarian efforts" in the separatist south, Washington will vote against multilateral loans to Sudan and consider downgrading or suspending diplomatic ties, the resolution says.

The United States will also try to prevent the government from using oil revenues to acquire weapons, and seek a U.N. Security Council resolution imposing an arms embargo; again, the rebels are exempt from the Americans' rules.

The legislation also authorizes the Administration to spend $100 million a year in the fiscal years of 2003, 2004 and 2005 to improve conditions in areas of Sudan not under government control. This irresponsibly links the humanitarian situation of northern Sudanese Arabs with the actions of their government, regardless of their lack of influence on a totalitarian regime. It also implies that their suffering is perhaps not as important to alleviate as those of the mostly Christian and animist south.

[The Sudan Peace Act] is direct meddling in another country's internal affairs . . . the [SPLA] now has no incentive to stick to the peace track.

Khartoum has branded the U.S. decision "unbalanced and unobjective," and urged Arab, Muslim and other parliaments to denounce it. "We are not an American state," said President Omar Al Bashir. He said the United States has "previously imposed sanctions on us and, if they strike us today, we will not succumb to them."

Foreign Minister Mustafa Osman Ismail added: "If the aim of this message is to add more pressure on the Sudanese government so that it can accept any kind of peace, then this step would only lead to a stalemate in the peace process. . . . The neutral role which we had been expecting from the U.S. administration regarding the peace process is turning out to be negative, and is biased in favor of the rebel movement."

A violation of Sudan's sovereignty

The Sudanese National Assembly called the bill "a flagrant violation of international law and a breach of Sudan's sovereignty," adding that it "makes the United States an international policeman that rules over the destinies of the peoples of the world."

This reaction is not surprising, given that this is direct meddling in another country's internal affairs (an increasingly commonplace U.S. strategy, particularly since the September 11 attacks), and that the Sudan People's Liberation Army (SPLA) now has no incentive to stick to the peace track.

On the contrary, the U.S. legislation gives the rebels a free reign, knowing that only the government's conduct will be the focus of American attention and reprisals.

As such, it does more to encourage war than peace. It is perhaps no coincidence that on the same day Bush signed the legislation, Khartoum reported that the SPLA violated a truce agreement reached just days earlier as a prelude to peace talks in Kenya by attacking three government positions, killing civilians and stealing cattle, a valuable food source in desperate times.

Despite the U.S. bill, Sudan's government seems to be standing firm. Army spokesman General Mohamed Beshir Suleiman said government forces repulsed the attacks and inflicted "heavy losses in lives and equipment." He added that Khartoum "will remain committed to all conventions and agreements, and will at the same time be committed to protecting positions against any aggression."

U.S. hypocrisy

Sadly, U.S. partiality in this conflict is not new. Washington condemned Sudan's government for quitting negotiations after the strategic town of Torit fell to the SPLA on September 1 [2002]. The fact that the rebels increased hostilities and captured a major town during peace talks went without rebuke, and rebel attacks since then have been met with similar silence from Washington.

The United States has also long provided humanitarian and financial aid solely to the rebels, drawing fire from governments and humanitarian groups for its one-sidedness.

This partiality is certainly not new to the region. One is reminded of U.S. claims of being an "honest broker" in Arab-Israeli peace talks, while simultaneously championing Israel's military superiority and economic well-being, and turning a blind eye to its daily violations of human rights and international law.

Despite the advantages granted to the rebels by the Sudan Peace Act, the SPLA would be wise to avoid unilateral hostilities and focus on negotiations. After all, the government, perhaps mindful of the suffering of its people and finally realizing the futility of ruling another by force, has never been more willing to make peace.

Under a framework deal reached in Kenya on July 20 [2003], Sudan's government granted the south the right to vote on full secession after six years of self-rule, during which they will be exempt from the Islamic law applied in the north. These are groundbreaking concessions that largely satisfy rebel demands and may herald an end to a conflict that has killed two million people and displaced twice that number.

12

The United States Should Lift Its Sanctions Against Libya

Ray Takeyh

Ray Takeyh is a professor at the National Defense University's Near East and South Asia Center.

The United States has regarded Libya as hostile to U.S. interests ever since Colonel Muammar al-Gadhafi seized power and instituted a socialist economy in the country in 1969. When a terrorist bomb brought down Pan Am Flight 103 over the village of Lockerbie, Scotland, on December 21, 1988, the United States blamed Libya for sponsoring the terrorists, and both the United Nations and the United States implemented an array of economic sanctions against the country. On August 15, 2003, Libya formally accepted responsibility for the Lockerbie bombing and agreed to pay $2.7 billion to the families of the victims as compensation. This gesture, along with Libya's economic reforms and Gadhafi's cooperation with the United States in the hunt for terrorists, suggest that sanctions against Libya have worked. Since Libya is no longer a state sponsor of terrorism, the sanctions against it should be lifted, and the United States should begin creating economic ties with the nation.

After 15 years of diplomatic wrangling, Libya has finally agreed to pay $2.7 billion to the families of the 270 victims of the Lockerbie bombing. The conclusion of this saga indicates an even more momentous development, namely Moammar Gaddafi's acceptance of international norms. It is time for the Bush administration to proclaim victory and begin the process of reintegrating the reforming rogue back into the community of nations.

In the years since he assumed power in 1969, Gaddafi has supported a wide variety of terrorist organizations and insurgencies that shared his disdain for the international order and its primary guardian, the United

States. Thus the Lockerbie bombing was part of Libya's prolonged involvement in the practice of terrorism. But a decade of multilateral sanctions and international isolation began to affect even this militant revolutionary, and led him gradually to abandon terrorism as a policy instrument. Even before this latest step, Gaddafi had begun distancing himself from his erstwhile terrorist allies, severing ties with radical Palestinian groups and closing the once notorious camps that trained a generation of terrorists.

> *Washington should acknowledge that the U.S.-led campaign to change Libyan policy has accomplished its original aims.*

Unlike many of his counterparts, the Libyan strongman viewed the post-9/11 war on terrorism as an opportunity to refurbish his image. The colonel condemned the attacks unequivocally, and Libya soon began cooperating with the United States by furnishing intelligence on the Libyan Fighting Islamic Group, a terrorist organization with links to Osama bin Laden [the leader of the terrorist organization al-Qaeda].

This is more than mere tactics; Gaddafi's recent rhetoric and behavior hint at a genuine ideological conversion. The collapse of the Soviet Union, a growing interest in Africa and an emerging disdain for Arab politics led him to offer a new vision for his restive nation. In a September 2000 speech commemorating the Libyan revolution, the colonel not only proclaimed the end of his anti-imperialist struggle but also suggested that it was time for cooperation with former antagonists. "Now is the era of economy, consumption, markets and investments. This is what unites people irrespective of language, religion and national identities," proclaimed Gaddafi to his startled audience.

U.S. skepticism

Washington has viewed this apparent transformation with understandable skepticism. Beyond terrorism, the United States also has concerns about Gaddafi's weapons-of-mass-destruction programs and his influence peddling in Africa. But the former issue seems overblown. With poor technological infrastructure and its sole nuclear facility—an aging Soviet-made research reactor—operating under supervision of the International Atomic Energy Agency, Libya represents a minimal threat to nuclear nonproliferation regimes. On the more vexing issue of chemical weapons, Gaddafi has intimated a desire to sign the Chemical Weapons Convention and should be pressed to do so.

The Libyan leader's African adventurism represents a more intricate problem. The United States views Libya's assistance to a variety of African autocrats as evidence of its "destructive role in perpetuating regional conflicts."

But in seeking allies and commercial advantage across the continent, Gaddafi has exerted constructive influences in some places, mediating regional crises and offering development aid in order to gain influence with dubious African leaders. Toward this end, the colonel has sought to resolve the conflicts in Congo, Sudan and the Horn of Africa, and was instrumental in crafting the 1999 cease-fire accord between Uganda and Congo. Although his efforts are often quixotic—for example, his proposed United States of Africa—his policy reflects a shift from one of relentless confrontation to a recognition of the possibilities of cooperation.

It is clear that Gaddafi's Africa policy is motivated more by economic opportunism than ideological militancy. He has aided the authoritarian president of Zimbabwe, Robert Mugabe, and recently ousted Liberian strongman Charles Taylor as a means of gaining access to their countries' valuable mining, agricultural and tourism industries. In the end, however, Libya's part in initiating or prolonging these conflicts is relatively minor, and it is dwarfed by the direct influence wielded by the continent's true power brokers, South Africa and Nigeria. More to the point, a sustained U.S. commitment to Africa would prove the most effective counter to Libya's efforts.

The United States should encourage reform

Rather than perpetuating its policy beyond its useful purpose, Washington should acknowledge that the U.S.-led campaign to change Libyan policy has accomplished its original aims. Given that Libya is no longer a state sponsor of terrorism, it should be formally removed from the terrorism list. Such a gesture would signal to other recalcitrant regimes that their isolation is not immutable and that abandoning terrorism can abolish the opprobrium that comes with being branded an outlaw state.

In the age of proliferation of weapons of mass destruction, the world cannot accept Gaddafi's renunciation of them at face value. But instead of maintaining unilateral sanctions, Washington should propose the phased establishment of diplomatic and trade ties in exchange for Libya's full compliance with all nonproliferation treaties.

The final Lockerbie compensation offer marked the triumph of a deliberate American policy pursued by three successive administrations. A Libyan state that once served as a model of how to deal with rogue states can now serve as a model of how to deal with a revolutionary regime weary of its isolation and ostracism.

13

The United States Should Not Lift Its Sanctions Against Libya

Nile Gardiner, James Phillips, and Peter Brookes

Nile Gardiner, James Phillips, and Peter Brookes are research fellows at the Heritage Foundation, a conservative think tank in Washington, D.C.

On August 15, 2003, Libya formally accepted responsibility for the terrorist bombing that brought down Pan Am Flight 103 over Lockerbie, Scotland, on December 21, 1988. Libya agreed to pay $2.7 billion to the families of the victims in compensation. The country's actions have prompted the United Nations to call for a lifting of the economic sanctions that have been in place against Libya since 1992. However, lifting the sanctions is a dangerous move because Libya is still a rogue nation that threatens the United States and international security. A longtime supporter of terrorists, Libya is also active in trying to develop chemical and biological weapons as well as ballistic missiles. Moreover, Libyan leader Colonel Muammar al-Gadhafi is still a dictator, and his regime is guilty of numerous ongoing human rights violations. Creating economic ties with Libya now would send a message to other rogue nations that the United States is willing to negotiate with state sponsors of terrorists.

The Libyan government has announced that it will pay $2.7 billion in compensation to the families of the 270 victims of the 1988 Pan Am Lockerbie bombing, including 189 Americans. The compensation offer is expected to result in a UN Security Council resolution calling for the lifting of sanctions against Tripoli, which have been in place since 1992 (the sanctions were suspended in 1999 after Libya surrendered two officials indicted for organizing the Lockerbie bombing). The resolution is likely to be sponsored by Britain; the Bush Administration has indicated that it may abstain rather than oppose it.

The lifting of sanctions on Libya at this time would be a grave mistake. Libya remains a growing threat to US national interests and international security. This would be appeasement of a brutal and dangerous regime, and would send completely the wrong message to other rogue regimes across the world.

Qadhafi denies responsibility

Under the Libyan offer, each victim is to receive $10 million: $4 million to be paid when UN sanctions are lifted; $4 million once US sanctions are lifted; and $2 million when the United States takes Libya off the State Department's list of state sponsors of terrorism.

Despite the compensation offer, Libya's head of state Colonel Muammar Qadhafi refuses to accept personal responsibility for the Lockerbie bombing, and continues to maintain his own innocence and that of his regime. The Libyan leader has a visceral hatred of the United States and as late as 1999 compared America to Nazi Germany, claiming, "Libya is a victim of American terrorism."

While Libya's offer of compensation is a step in the right direction, it would be wrong for the Bush Administration to accede to Libyan demands that this be linked to the lifting of UN or US sanctions and the removal of Libya from the State Department's list of state sponsors of terrorism. This would be appeasement of a brutal and dangerous regime, and would send completely the wrong message to other rogue regimes across the world. It would undermine many of the steps taken by the United States since September 11 to combat the threat posed by rogue states. There should be no negotiation with terrorist regimes.

There are several key reasons why the United States should oppose the UN lifting of sanctions against Libya, as well as the lifting of US sanctions.

Weapons of mass destruction

Despite growing international concern, Libya is attempting to develop weapons of mass destruction. Undersecretary of State for Arms Control and International Security John Bolton has described Libya as a "rogue state" and a major potential threat to international security.

In a 2002 speech to the Heritage Foundation, Bolton warned that Libya was continuing to build up its chemical and biological weapons programs. The Libyans are also actively trying to develop their ballistic missile program, with the assistance of North Korea, China, Serbia and India. If Libya continues to receive international assistance, it may achieve extended-range SCUD or Medium Range Ballistic Missile capability. In addition, according to Bolton, "Tripoli's nuclear infrastructure remains of concern," although Tripoli would require significant international assistance in order to acquire a nuclear weapon.

Support for international terrorism and African dictators

Libya is one of seven regimes listed by the State Department as state sponsors of terrorism. The country has a long history of support for terrorist groups in the Middle East and more than thirty terrorist groups worldwide. Libya provided arms, funding, and training for a wide variety of

Palestinian terrorist groups (Fatah, the Palestine Liberation Front, the Democratic Front for the Liberation of Palestine, the Popular Front for the Liberation of Palestine, the Popular Front for the Liberation of Palestine-General Command, and the Abu Nidal group), as well as the Kurdistan Workers Party, the Colombian terrorist group M19, the Red Brigades in Italy, and assorted other terrorist groups in Japan, Turkey, Northern Ireland, Thailand and elsewhere.

Libya was caught red-handed sponsoring a terrorist attack against Americans in 1986, when it bombed a German discotheque frequented by American servicemen, killing two Americans. The Reagan Administration retaliated by bombing Libyan targets on April 15, 1986, narrowly missing Qadhafi himself. Although Libya has not been caught red-handed in launching terrorist attacks in recent years, it has not closed down all of its terrorist training camps and could resume its terrorist activities as soon as it finds it convenient to do so.

There should be no negotiation with terrorist regimes.

In addition to its involvement in the Lockerbie bombing, Libya is also responsible for the 1989 bombing of a French passenger jet in Niger, which killed 170 people. A French court convicted in absentia six Libyans, including the brother in law of Colonel Qadhafi, for carrying out the bombing. Libya offered to pay a paltry $33 million in compensation to the families.

Colonel Qadhafi has for many years suffered from delusions of grandeur regarding his position on the international stage, and sees himself as the natural leader of a future United States of Africa. In order to advance this goal he has played an important role in propping up some of the continent's worst dictators, whom he sees as his natural allies.

Tripoli played a prominent role for example in arming and training former President Charles Taylor of Liberia. As recently as July [2003], Taylor is reported to have visited Libya in order to restock on arms and ammunition.

Appalling human rights record

Despite its ludicrous chairmanship of the UN Commission on Human Rights, Libya remains one of the most repressive regimes in the world, along with North Korea and Iran.

Since coming to power in 1969, Colonel Qadaffi has built up a reputation as one of Africa's most brutal and thuggish dictators. As the State Department's annual report on 'Human Rights Practices' points out, the Libyan regime suppresses domestic opposition, tortures prisoners, arbitrarily arrests and detains its citizens, and refuses detainees a fair public trial. It also greatly restricts freedom of speech, press, assembly and religion, and is even accused of trafficking in human slavery.

Libya's record on economic freedom is equally poor. According to the Heritage Foundation/Wall Street Journal *Index of Economic Freedom*, Libya's quasi-Marxist economy is the fifth most repressive in the world, and the least free in the whole of Africa with the exception of Zimbabwe.

Key recommendations:

- The Bush Administration should oppose both the lifting of United Nations sanctions and US sanctions against Libya. The lifting of either would not serve the US national interest, and would set a dangerous precedent.
- Libya should remain on the State Department list of state supporters of terrorism until it has closed its terrorist training camps, punished the officials involved in supporting terrorism, and cooperated in dismantling the terrorist groups that it formerly supported.
- Colonel Qadhafi should continue to be held accountable for the Lockerbie bombing and other terrorist acts.
- The US should not restore diplomatic relations with Tripoli until it has satisfactorily proven that it has permanently halted its support of terrorism.
- Washington must increase pressure on Libya to sign the Chemical Weapons Convention (CWC) and Biological Weapons Convention (BWC) and open its biological and chemical facilities to international inspection.
- The US should pressure China, India, Serbia and North Korea to halt nuclear cooperation with Libya.
- The United States must reserve the right to use military force against the Libyan regime if it continues to act as a state sponsor of terrorism or poses a threat to US and international security.

Don't lift sanctions

The lifting of sanctions on Libya at this time would be a grave mistake. Libya remains a growing threat to US national interests and international security. The suspension of UN sanctions against Tripoli has enabled Libya to step up its biological, chemical and ballistic missile programs. A total lifting of UN and US sanctions could have disastrous results and would send entirely the wrong message to other rogue regimes.

Organizations to Contact

The editors have compiled the following list of organizations concerned with the issues debated in this book. The descriptions are derived from materials provided by the organizations. All have publications or information available for interested readers. The list was compiled on the date of publication of the present volume; the information provided here may change. Be aware that many organizations take several weeks or longer to respond to inquiries, so allow as much time as possible.

American Enterprise Institute (AEI)
1150 Seventeenth St. NW, Washington, DC 20036
website: www.aei.org

AEI is a think tank based in Washington, D.C., whose members support a strong and well-funded military and are "hawkish" in regard to America's war on terrorism. AEI publishes the magazine *American Enterprise*. Other publications include papers "Fighting Terror: Lessons and Implications from the Iraqi Theater" and "Brave New World: An Enduring Pax Americana."

Brookings Institution
1775 Massachusetts Ave. NW, Washington, DC 20036
(202) 797-6000 • fax: (202) 797-6004
e-mail: brookinfo@brook.edu • website: www.brook.edu

Founded in 1927, the institution conducts research and analyzes global events and their impact on the United States and U.S. foreign policy. It publishes the *Brookings Review* quarterly as well as numerous books and research papers on foreign policy. Numerous reports on foreign policy and rogue nations are available on the institution's website, including *The New National Security Strategy and Preemption* and *A "Master" Plan to Deal with North Korea*.

Cato Institute
1000 Massachusetts Ave. NW, Washington, DC 20001-5403
(202) 842-0200 • fax: (202) 842-3490
website: www.cato.org

The institute is a libertarian public policy research foundation dedicated to peace and limited government intervention in foreign affairs. It publishes numerous reports and periodicals, including *Policy Analysis* and *Cato Policy Review*, both of which discuss U.S. policy in regional conflicts. CATO members have published numerous analysis and opinion pieces opposing both the U.S. invasion of Iraq and the use of force against other nations thought to support terrorism.

Center for Strategic and International Studies (CSIS)
1800 K St. NW, Washington, DC 20006
(202) 887-0200 • fax: (202) 775-3199
website: www.csis.org

CSIS is a public policy research institution that specializes in the areas of U.S. domestic and foreign policy, national security, and economic policy. The center analyzes world crisis situations and recommends U.S. military and defense policies. Its publications include the journal *The Washington Quarterly* and the reports *Change and Challenge on the Korean Peninsula: Developments, Trends, and Issues* and *Combating Chemical, Biological, Radiological, and Nuclear Terrorism: A Comprehensive Strategy.*

Council on Foreign Relations
58 E. 68th St., New York, NY 10021
(212) 434-9400 • fax: (212) 986-2984
website: www.cfr.org

The council specializes in foreign affairs and studies the international aspects of American political and economic policies and problems. Its journal *Foreign Affairs*, published five times a year, includes analyses of current conflicts around the world. Articles and op-ed pieces by CFR members are available on its website, along with the report *A New National Security Strategy in an Age of Terrorists, Tyrants, and Weapons of Mass Destruction.*

Foreign Policy Association (FPA)
470 Park Ave. South, 2nd Fl., New York, NY 10016
(212) 481-8100 • fax: (212) 481-9275
e-mail: info@fpa.org • website: www.fpa.org

FPA is a nonprofit organization that believes a concerned and informed public is the foundation for an effective foreign policy. Publications such as the annual *Great Decisions* briefing book and the quarterly *Headline Series* review U.S. foreign policy issues in China, the Persian Gulf and the Middle East, and Africa. FPA's *Global Q & A* series offers interviews with leading U.S. and foreign officials on issues concerning the Middle East, intelligence gathering, weapons of mass destruction, and military and diplomatic initiatives.

Global Exchange
2017 Mission St., #303, San Francisco, CA 94110
(415) 255-7296 • fax: (415) 255-7498
website: www.globalexchange.org

Global Exchange is a human rights organization that exposes economic and political injustice around the world. In response to such injustices, the organization supports education, activism, and a noninterventionist U.S. foreign policy. The organization believes that the terrorist attacks of September 11 do not justify U.S. retaliation against civilian populations. It opposed the U.S. invasions of Afghanistan and Iraq and supports an end to the trade embargo against Cuba. It publishes *Global Exchanges* quarterly.

Heritage Foundation
214 Massachusetts Ave. NE, Washington, DC 20002-4999
(800) 544-4843 • (202) 546-4400 • fax: (202) 544-6979
e-mail: pubs@heritage.org • website: www.heritage.org

The foundation is a public policy research institute that advocates limited government and the free-market system. The foundation publishes the quarterly *Policy Review* as well as monographs, books, and papers supporting U.S. noninterventionism. Heritage publications on U.S. foreign policy include

Why U.S. Troops Should Not Be Sent to Liberia, Iran: Revolting Against the Revolution?, and *Resolving the North Korean Nuclear Issue.*

Resource Center for Nonviolence
515 Broadway, Santa Cruz, CA 95060
(831) 423-1626 • fax: (831) 423-8716
e-mail: rcnv@rcnv.org • website: www.rcnv.org

The Resource Center for Nonviolence was founded in 1976 and promotes nonviolence as a force for personal and social change. It opposed the war in Iraq and supports peace protests to help prevent future U.S. military actions. The center provides speakers, workshops, leadership development, and nonviolence training programs and also publishes a newsletter, *Center Report*, twice a year.

United Nations Association of the United States of America
801 Second Ave., New York, NY 10017
(212) 907-1300
website: www.unausa.org

The association is a nonpartisan, nonprofit research organization dedicated to strengthening both the United Nations and U.S. participation in the council. Its publications include the bimonthly newspaper the *Interdependent* and the reports *Rebuilding Iraq: How the United States and United Nations Can Work Together*, and *The Use of Force, Legitimacy, and the U.N. Charter.*

U.S. Department of State
2201 C St. NW, Washington, DC 20520
website: www.state.gov

The State Department is a federal agency that advises the president on the formulation and execution of foreign policy. The Office of Counterterrorism publishes the annual report *Patterns of Global Terrorism*, which lists the nations that the United States has designated as state sponsors of terrorism; a list of United States's most wanted terrorists; and pages providing background information on every country in the world.

Bibliography

Books

Andrew J. Bacevich — *American Empire: The Realities and Consequences of U.S. Diplomacy*. Cambridge, MA: Harvard University Press, 2002.

William Blum — *Rogue State: A Guide to the World's Only Superpower*. Monroe, ME: Common Courage Press, 2000.

Max Boot — *The Savage Wars of Peace: Small Wars and the Rise of American Power*. New York: Basic Books, 2002.

Fraser Cameron — *U.S. Foreign Policy After the Cold War: Global Hegemon or Reluctant Sheriff?* New York: Routledge, 2002.

Gabriel Kolko — *Another Century of War?* New York: New Press, 2002.

Michael A. Ledeen — *The War Against the Terror Masters: Why It Happened. Where We Are Now. How We'll Win*. New York: St. Martin's Press, 2002.

Robert Litwak — *Rogue States and U.S. Foreign Policy: Containment After the Cold War*. Washington, DC: Woodrow Wilson Center Press, 2000.

Richard Mintzer — *Keeping the Peace: The U.S. Military Responds to Terror*. New York: Chelsea House, 2002.

Paul R. Pillar — *Terrorism and U.S. Foreign Policy*. Washington, DC: Brookings Institution Press, 2001.

Howard Zinn — *Terrorism and War*. New York: Seven Stories Press, 2002.

Periodicals

America — "The Bush Doctrine," March 18, 2002.

Pascal Boniface — "What Justifies Regime Change?" *Washington Quarterly*, Summer 2003.

Max Boot — "The Case for American Empire," *Weekly Standard*, October 15, 2001.

George W. Bush — "The 2002 State of the Union: We Will See Freedom's Victory," *Vital Speeches of the Day*, February 15, 2002.

Massimo Calabresi — "The Next WMD Crisis: New Evidence Suggests That North Korea Is Advancing Its Nuclear-Weapons Plans. What Can the U.S. Do?" *Time*, July 28, 2003.

Tony Carnes — "The Bush Doctrine: The Moral Vision That Launched the Iraq War Has Been Quietly Growing in the President's Inner Circle," *Christianity Today*, May 2003.

David Cortright — "Proposed: A More Effective and Just Response to Terrorism," *USA Today*, January 2002.

Economist — "After Iraq; Proliferation," May 31, 2002.

Economist — "Stuck on the Axis of Evil?: Iran's Confused Foreign Policy," January 18, 2003.

Craig Eisendrath — "U.S. Foreign Policy After September 11," *USA Today*, May 2002.

Free Inquiry — "The War Against Iraq. (The Immorality of)," Spring 2003.

Frank J. Gaffney Jr. and Jon B. Wolfsthal — "Symposium: Should the United States Target Iraq?" *Insight on the News*, May 6, 2002.

William Galston — "Perils of Preemptive War: Why America's Place in the World Will Shift—for Worse—If We Attack Iraq," *American Prospect*, September 23, 2002.

Mark Helprin — "Phony War: The President's Policy Does Not Comport with the Valor and Sacrifice of His Troops," *National Review*, April 22, 2002.

Stanley Hoffman — "The High and the Mighty: Bush's National-Security Doctrine and the New American Hubris," *American Prospect*, January 13, 2003.

Peter Huessey and Paul Craig Roberts — "Symposium: Will Pre-Emptive War, Such as in Iraq, Make the United States Safer in the Long Term?" *Insight on the News*, April 29, 2003.

Paul Johnson — "From 'the Evil Empire' to 'the Empire for Liberty,'" *New Criterion*, June 2003.

Robert D. Kaplan — "Supremacy by Stealth: Ten Rules for Managing the World," *Atlantic Monthly*, July/August 2003.

Julie Kosterlitz — "Empire Strikes Back," *National Journal*, December 14, 2002.

Michael Ledeen and James Miskel — "Symposium: Should the United States Seek Regime Change in Syria with Saddam Hussein's Defeat?" *Insight on the News*, July 8, 2003.

Richard Lowry — "A View to a Kill: Assassination in War and Peace," *National Review*, March 11, 2002.

Newsweek — "A Wide World of Trouble: While Bush Pushes War Against Iraq, New Threats Loom from Al Qaeda and North Korea. Can We Fight on All These Fronts?" October 28, 2002.

Thomas Omestad and Kenneth T. Walsh — "Power and Peril," *U.S. News & World Report*, May 5, 2003.

Sharif Shuja — "North Korea and the Nuclear Threat," *Contemporary Review*, May 2003.

Jack Spencer — "Do Iraq, Iran, and North Korea Truly Constitute an Axis of Evil?" *USA Today*, May 2002.

Jay Tolson   "The New American Empire?" *U.S. News & World Report*, January 13, 2003.

World Watch   "Weapons of Mass Distraction," July/August 2003.

Websites

Antiwar.com
www.antiwar.com

This site lists dozens of antiwar viewpoints written by Antiwar.com columnists, as well as links to antiwar viewpoints on other sites.

Foreign Policy in Focus
www.fpif.org

FPIF members publish online articles about the war on terrorism and other foreign policy topics.

International Policy Institute for Counter-Terrorism
www.ict.org.il

The institute is an Israeli-based research organization. Its website offers profiles of terrorist organizations, a database of worldwide terrorist attacks, and numerous analysis articles on state-sponsored terrorism.

Terrorism Research Center
www.terrorism.com

This site features essays and thought pieces on current issues, as well as links to other terrorism documents, research, and resources.

Index